"*The Toad of Dawn* offers another piece of the consciousness puzzle: 5-MeO-DMT, aka the Godhead. Dr. Rettig's DMT multiverse unravels novel '*reality tunnels*' in the search for meaning from the macro to micro. In pure gonzo style, his personal hero's journey provides a context to explore the sacrament's history, plant intelligence, emerging culture, future consciousness, and more."
—MITCH SCHULTZ, Film Producer of *DMT: The Spirit Molecule*

"This powerful and important story is set within the life challenges of one modern man, yet echoes profoundly the ancient wisdom regarding sacred use of visionary substances."
—BROOKE MEDICINE EAGLE, Author of *Buffalo Woman Comes Singing*

"Dr. Octavio Rettig helps bring on the dawn of a consciously evolved humanity as he partners with one of the most powerful natural healing agents available on this good Earth. This is the *Toad of Dawn*. He has helped rejuvenate the spirits of thousands of people with his medicine work."
—ALEXANDER GEORGE WARD, Shamanic Artist, Illustrator of *Ayahuasca Jungle Visions*

The Toad of Dawn

5-MeO-DMT
and the Rise of Cosmic Consciousness

Dr. Octavio Rettig Hinojosa

Introduction by Rak Razam

DIVINE
ARTS

Published by DIVINE ARTS
DivineArtsMedia.com

An imprint of Michael Wiese Productions
12400 Ventura Blvd. #1111
Studio City, CA 91604
(818) 379-8799, (818) 986-3408 (FAX)

Translator: Municor
Editors: Geraldine Overton and Gary Sunshine
Layout artist: William Morosi
Cover Design: John Brenner
Cover Photo: Pen Densham
Toad Sculpture Courtesy of Thomas Schoos
Fractal Art by Lenora Clark www.theartoflenoraclark.com
Printed by McNaughton & Gunn, Inc., Saline, Michigan

Note to the Reader: The information provided in this book is for educational, historical, and cultural interest only and should not be construed as advocacy for the use or ingestion of 5-MeO-DMT or other psychedelics. Neither the author nor the publisher assumes any responsibility for physical, psychological, or social consequences resulting from the ingestion of these substances or their derivatives.

Text set in 10-point Columbus MT with headings in 12-point AT Classic

Library of Congress Cataloging-in-Publication Data

Names: Rettig Hinojosa, Octavio, 1979- author.
Title: The toad of dawn : 5-MeO-DMT and the Rise of Cosmic Consciousness /
  Dr. Octavio Rettig Hinojosa.
Description: Studio City, CA : Divine Arts, [2016]
Identifiers: LCCN 2015024548| ISBN 9781611250466 (paperback) | ISBN
  9781611250473
Subjects: LCSH: Dimethyltryptamine. | Pineal gland--Secretions. | Mysticism.
  | Bufonidae. | BISAC: BODY, MIND & SPIRIT / Healing / General. | SOCIAL
  SCIENCE / Anthropology / General. | BODY, MIND & SPIRIT / Mysticism.
Classification: LCC RM666.D564 R48 2016 | DDC 615.7883--dc23
LC record available at http://lccn.loc.gov/2015024548

Printed on Recycled Stock

CONTENTS

PART TWO:
FULL DISCLOSURE

PART THREE:
OTAC IN THE WORLD

ACKNOWLEDGMENTS

First, I would like to give thanks to God for all that is, to Nature, and to the wisdom of plants, animals, and all of creation.

To Bertha, for all her eternal and unconditional love, for her support and example, and for her words of encouragement. I love you, beautiful mother. To my father, who is now with God, and who is doubtless out there somewhere still being his gracious self. Blessed you be, Werner Rafael Rettig Martorell. To my brother, David, for his example and leadership. I admire you truly.

To my uncle, Jose Francisco Hinojosa, archeologist, who helped me see life in a different way, who kindled within me a love for history and pre-Columbian mythology. To my godfather, Hector Rigoberto Hinojosa, for his work and motivation; you taught me to work at an early age and to do things right the first time. To Luis Guillermo Hinojosa, for his teachings and nobility, and for showing me that we can in fact change. To Salvador, for his perseverance and tenacity. You are the best example of persistence. And to Licho, for his affection. It is what you are: Love.

To Paul Rettig Martorell; my cousins, Hilda and Oswaldo; and my half-brothers, Werner and Ivar.

To my children, Edsel and Salvia. You are my reason for being.

To Sugeli and Ceci, for the gifts that have been received and the experiences lived. To Luis Enrique Gonzalez, for keeping history close and helping me tell the truth.

To my dearest friends, teachers and fellow travelers, Mr. Juan Flores Meza and Mr. Amando Hernandez Brizuela.

To the faculty and alumni of the Medicine Field of the University of Guadalajara.

The Seri Nation and the elders of the community. Specially to Grandpa Pancho (Jose Francisco Barnett Astorga).

To the many colorful characters who live on this Earth and whom I have had the honor of sharing experiences with.

To the plants, for their innumerable teachings and for allowing me to hear them. And to all those molecules that taught me to feel magic and remember who we are; you lead me to spiritual awakening and understanding. To all the rocks in my path that paved the road to oblivion, which became my teacher. To consciousness, wisdom, perseverance, and victory; we are one. And to the muses, sources of the creative inspiration that move my body from within.

Thanks to the work and research of:

William James (1842–1910)
Aldous Huxley (1894–1963)
R. Gordon Wasson (1898–1986)
Albert Hofmann (1906–2008)
William S. Burroughs (1924–1997)
Ken Kesey (1935–2001)
Terence McKenna (1946–2000)
Richard Evan Schultes (1915–2001)
Alexander "Sasha" Shulgin (1925–2014)

Doctors Guillermo Rodríguez, Eduardo López Mireles, Francisco Delgado Sánchez, Amed Arturo Barnez Tanori, and quite specifically Doctor Gerry, for helping me meet my goals while swimming upstream.

To all those who directly or indirectly contributed to the completion of this work.

And more than anyone else, thanks to you, the reader, for receiving the messages within these lines. Thank you.

PROLOGUE:

WE HAVE ARRIVED: IT IS HERE AND NOW

There exists a State of Being where microcosm and macrocosm, sky and Earth, merge into a cosmic embrace; it is here and now that past, present, and future occur at once, in perfect sync, beyond linear time and space. It is where One is All and All are One. It is Alpha and Omega, the beginning and end of the eternal film that is life in constant transformation.

To live is to transcend the terrifying and tragic ancient misconception popularly known as death. Death is temporary and spatial; life is by nature eternal.

There exists a State of Being where death ceases to exist: here and now. I must confess that I could not write the prologue to this book without the generosity of Dr. Octavio Rettig, author of this book. It was he who introduced me to the ancestral medicine of the *Bufo alvarius* toad of the

Sonoran Desert, where it is affectionately known simply as El Sapito ("little toad"). Even so, it is clear to me that there are no words to describe what it means to transcend time and space and reach the point of here and now.

We have arrived; it is here and now. We are at the threshold of Heaven on Earth. Everything is in perfect sync. The Light Source exists, and it is pure love. The words "I am God integrating" may sound vague, but such is an example of what one may hear within while regaining consciousness. The feeling reminds me of a song by the Mexican group Caifanes: "Let's travel to the sky to see eternity."

This book originated in a busy doctor's handwriting on pages saturated, jammed, with hallucinatory experiences that reach beyond any doctor's office anywhere. Just as Albert Einstein said, "Theory is killed sooner or later by experience."

This is the story of a doctor, Octavio, who became the worst patient ever, with the ultimate aim to achieve a personal conversation with reality and to find his path to the light by means of an ancient treasure guarded for centuries: the toad called Otac in the language of the Seris Indians of Sonora, silent guardians of a treasure hidden inside a secret open to the cosmos.

To read the adventures that Octavio has lived, each more fantastic than the last, is like entering a film with such a wonderful script it is difficult to accept as real. We each carry old beliefs that we cannot accept as true anything unproven by the five senses. And this book is certainly "sense-less" in the view of conventional logic. This information is an earthquake, thrilling and oscillating, demolishing old structures imposed on us by fear of the unknown.

For Octavio, modern society is sick with fear, selfishness, and consumerism. At a deep level, it is addicted to discomfort and suffering. To keep the masses sick and obedient is, first of all, an enormous business. Science is a stock market service whose only objective is to maximize profits. The last thing the market of consumerism wants is for people to heal; profits grow at the same rate that our state of illness worsens. This is why more and more syndromes, disorders, and diseases are being fabricated by mass media; we are all affected by these toxic symptoms. It is as if suddenly life has become a chronic disease and the only effective medicines, albeit palliative, are those sold in pharmacies by prescription. Or worse, the synthetic drugs handed out like aspirin on the street corners of big cities intoxicated with stress, hurry, and selfishness. Consumerism is an illness that prescribes for us this business plan: buy death in convenient installments throughout your life.

If anyone knows firsthand about addiction to social drugs, it is our very own Octavio Rettig. This book narrates the path of a sick doctor poisoned by professional ego, who through a crack cocaine addiction touched personal rock bottom, reaching the darkest places in himself. From that depth he was able to reemerge, finally reaching the light at the end of the tunnel. All paths lead to enlightenment, say the grandparent guardians of our deepest roots. Every addiction is, in fact, a spiritual search. Of course, there is no advantage to reaching rock bottom unless we can get back up, regaining our balance despite everything. Our journey becomes truth incarnate, an example of self-love, the human spirit at its finest.

This book is the autobiography of Dr. Octavio Rettig, who ceased being sick in order to become, Little Toad in hand, medicine man for the whole planet. His is the story of life and spiritual transformation in the genesis of a new world.

We have arrived. It is here and now.

Santiago Pando
The Tree House, Leones Desert
May 2013

Introduction:

Into the Light

Thursday April 2, 2015

The day before Easter. It's near midday and the noonday sun is beating down through clouds as I stand, feet spread-eagled, hands reaching up to embrace the sky, my body a bridge between heaven and earth. In front of me the solid gravity of Mt. Jerusalem, Northern NSW, Australia, a dense foliage of trees protruding from the skin of the mountain, the earth and rock lovers whispering to the sun. I stare at the uppermost tree crowning this leviathan spirit as the beaming, mischievous smile of Dr. Octavio Rettig moves toward me. His eyes are deep pools as he holds a small glass pipe up to my lips, lights it, and commands me to breathe in: slowly, slowly, that's it you're almost there, a little bit more, almost there, more, more... that's it! Now inhale deeply and *hold it...!*

Consciousness unfolds like a lotus petal into a white, white pool of becoming... everything is here and it swallows me whole, the drop returns to the ocean and there is no longer an *I* left to remember being separate... I'm fading in and out of the white, drowning in the remembrance, and what's left of my ego is panicking, split apart, bleeding soul stretched between all points in the space-time singularity — and at that exact moment, I am held.

It's not the shaman, not Octavio, my dear, dear brother, tending to my physical form as it collapses to the ground in the noonday sun, blessing it with his *icaro* songs and smoothing out my energetic body with his rattle. No, it's the others. I can feel, not see, their silhouetted light body forms around me — guardian spirits? Ancestors? Fellow shaman brothers, masculine, ancient, old and wizened like Shipibo *curanderos*... And they gently hold an arm, touch a shoulder, adjust my pineal third eye with the cool mint touch of ease; they hold me and they love me and support me as I come back from the fullness, the awe-full ness of the ALL, till my Eye can remember where I am again, what I am again:

Between my eyes my pineal literally pops, and it bursts the golden white seed-juice of the light, and the liquid is pure LOVE, unconditional love. It becomes a waterfall that thunders down my throat and I'm drowning on the inside, drowning in the purest of the pure white light LOVE that is ALL THERE IS... And I REMEMBER.... I remember where I am, what I am, what IT IS! A cascade of 5-MeO-DMT washes through my mind-body-soul, de-armoring, releasing, remembering....

And I know: my shaman brothers are here, all of them holding me up and supporting me and joyfully welcoming me home and to the MISSION I am on and we are on and it is fluid translinguistic YES YES YES this is the moment JOIN US! We are all doing this together you are protected you are loved you are joy you are God You Am I Am You Am I... This is the WORK and this is all is in flow THIS IS HAPPENING AND YOU ARE SUPPORTED and I'm just so fucking full of joy... A lifetime of wounds, insecurities, broken lines in my energetic template are healed in this crucible and reforged anew. And then the universe opens up and I drink it in....

That single superglue gestalt consciousness that is both everything interconnected and one thing enters me and speaks through me, glossolalia spaceluv, and that sound: this is how you navigate. This is how the universe steers. This is how we get to where we need to be.

I open my eyes and Octavio is there, chanting, smiling, loving, and my heart beats with this man. Our paths are entwined, and we do this work together, entangled, all of us that have been activated by this medicine, entangled on the quantum level where we are all One.

Thursday July 16, 2015

The wheel comes full circle, and I am back in the melt with Octavio, filming for a documentary series, *Shamans of the Global Village,* about his work with the Sonoran Desert toad. My crew and I have been welcomed to the Seri tribe, here in Sonora, Mexico, the desert heartland of this medicine. We have watched Octavio work with the indigenous youth of the tribe, helping heal addictions; we have been on the hunt for the *Bufo alvarius* toad in the Seri reserve, under the permission of the elders. We have milked the toad and watched the glistening milky jism glinting in the light like snowflakes from heaven, drying on a sheet of glass. And we have, unprecedentedly, been accompanied by Antonio, the Chief of the Seri, and Chapo, the village shaman, to the sacred Tiburon Island, where our ceremony unfolds.

One by one our Western guests are broken upon the shores of heaven. Octavio is dressed in a red ceremonial Seri shirt and pants, like a Mexican Elvis, shaking his rattle and singing the ancient Seri chants to his patients. We are all dressed in white, standing around a rock circle, holding space for the deep work that is to come and the One who goes in. The afternoon sun beats down, the crash of waves backbeats our ceremony, and we are immersed in this sacred space, far from the eyes of man.

I have learnt a deep respect for Octavio, and the way he works with this medicine, on the earth, outside in nature, where a full release can be held. I work by his side, splashing water into the nose and mouths of the seekers as he commands, watching, absorbing the lessons from him, his chants seeping into my unconscious. And one by one we all go in, under, into, yes... We die and are reborn, shattered by the power of the toad, and rewoven like shards of light. And then it's time.

It's dusk and the sun is setting as Octavio holds the pipe to my lips once more. And I remember the first time, and my four brother shaman spirits. And I look over and realize: last time is this time. Inside out, here and now, those four shamans are with me now: Octavio; Leo, our guide; Antonio, the village chief; and Chapo, dear Chapo, the octogenarian Seri shaman with the eyes of a child, the one who laughs and whose eyes glisten with the joy of each moment, who reminds us in gleeful tones as he whoops the sky: God is here. These are the four I felt with me before, and they assume the physical configuration around me as I go in again....

I'm staring at the sun. It wavers in the last gasp of afternoon haze as the magic moment hits, all of us focused on this perfect NOW. Octavio lights the pipe and the toad flakes burn and turn to smoke and I hold it in my lungs for as long as I can, slow and steady until I am totally full. The screen of my vision deepens behind an opaque screen, a veil parts as I stare at the sun without fear or harm and gaze deeply into the light. My pineal is buzzing as the smoke suffuses deep into me, and the light is all, and the breath within me curls down deep and I forget I even have to breathe… And IT is ON.

The Oneness is like a waterfall that comes from every direction at once, from within the center of the atom and the heart of all things and it is ON and ON and ON with such force, such loving force radiating outward everywherewhichwhen all at once.…

It's as if the entire reality grid is a universal Photoshop file, with millions of fractal layers: the wind, the sun, the earth under my feet, the crash of waves, the smile of Jewelli, my beloved, in the circle, the faces of my friends around, the rattle of the shaman, the wise Yoda face of Chapo my medicine man-child; all of these and so much more, including the holographic flow of moments that led up to this now, all of this, is full of spirit, and spirits. And all of these spirits are consensually IN on the whole thing; we are all connected. And the spirits are breathing through me, and the entire universe is like a cloak that I wear.

The universal cloak channels and radiates the fractal holographic spacetime continuum in and around me, through me, and the distributed consciousness of this frequency is TOO MUCH. It shatters the illusion of separateness, of ego and individuality, and I want it all to stop. I command it all to stop, not forever; what I'm saying in my clumsy language of engaging with the process on the psychic level is: I remember where I am. I understand. I know we are ALL ONE. I can feel you my brothers and sisters, spiritual beings, fellow shamans, and STOP. It's too much. Tweak it, slow it down, okay. I'm doing it, I'm ready, and ... not... now. I need to establish my boundaries, my sense of control of the uncontrollable. And this is the first ten seconds.

All right. Let's GO.

Protocol permissions established. Ballast engaged. Find the center within the cyclone. Claim my power and then... I fall to the ground under the gravity of love, rolling around, somatic body anchoring the enormous intense presence of the Source at the center of all things that radiates out from my every atom; all of that is and how I cope. It's the arrival of that energy into the vessel of my being, my temple, and it needs to express itself. And Octavio's chants and songs and shaman's rattle is a pure joy to my activated being, they are codes back to the Source as I reverberate and ripple and weave....

The ALL is ONE and I feel that tangibly, so much more than these words: I can FEEL the ALL fractaling outward into the universe, and I am not just connected to this current, I AM this current, and it is anchored in me in this moment, and the next, and the next, and the next, the eternal moment. My hands spontaneously form mudras to hold and channel the energy as I break into unbridled glossolalia and the spirits pour through me, sacred sound being born.

And my superconscious is conscious on multidimensional levels; everything I do has an equal and opposite reaction, so my cry moves my body and I roll with the sound and feel the caress of the sand and the earth grounding me as energy lightnings through my body. And that moment fractals into the next, holy holy holy holy and I kiss the dirt and it covers my face and the earth is aware and consensual in that moment, and it too is blessing me with its touch. Each thing I do is a blessing. Everything I am is a prayer. And it covers me and becomes me. And I spit and I cry and I laugh and I joy and I realize I AM IT.

SHAZAM!!!

And spirit breaks through my throat and into sound once more, a cacophony of spirit-sound, raining glossolalia-joy, gracias back to the Maker in each moment. And each of these fractal Photoshop layers is in perfect radiating superunion divinity. This is how the Source feels in the web of life as it becomes, the sacred hosted in the flesh of the world, the Word conjugated and holy vibration passing through our atomic selves, pulsing, pulsing, pulsing....

And my dear brother Octavio is still holding space, shamanizing over me, and Antonio is chanting with him and shaking his rattle, and Chapo is lifting his arms to the sky and laughing like a child, and this is IT and this is IT and this is IT and IT and IT and IT... Join us!

Then a perfect synchronicity moment: I remember this space where we are ALL ONE, this feeling of interconnectedness, this feeling of unity and weaving between us in harmonic resonance. And again, like before, always, now: Octavio splashes fresh water on my face, down my lips and curling into my nose to kickstart the breathing reflex. Water also hits my eyes, and inside, the seed of my pineal bursts once more with the golden juice of light perfectly synchronized with the splash of water on the outside, the pure unbroken crystalline vibration of LOVE. A Godgasm from the Source flowing through the portal of my being, bathing me in unconditional liquidlove. And the grace, the perfection of this moment… every domino moment, every fractal breath…

I walk toward the water, laughing, smiling, loving, wading in, my harmonica in one hand, and I am baptized in the holy, holy waters. The harmonica fills with water and as I shake it out I overflow with joy and water and love and understanding. I breathe out and a sharp, pure harmonica note bursts into the air, and the clouds billow overhead and entwine with the sun, and I look back at the shore, at the sacred land of Tiburon Island.

When we arrived on the island I had asked the spirits of this place to protect us, to strengthen us, to guide us, to love us. And I feel that in this space, in the rustling buzzing sacred power of this island, we were held, and initiated. And I could finally fully let go, fully embody this medicine, this being, the One that wears the universe as its skin. I was permissioned to fully become, and to be, because of all of you, all of US, and all that is, conspired to produce that moment.

This is the sacredness. This is the power. This is the medicine that Octavio Rettig brings to the world, wrapped in the chants, the power songs, his style of shamanizing, the deepest of healings and the deepest of openings that he holds space for. Great Spirit works through him.

I stand by this man. I fall with him. I rise with him. I salute him and the sacred work he does, and I say: if you feel the call, answer it. A song deep within us is asking to be sung.

Rise up and open your hearts, BE the song. Let it shine across the world, for the Dawn of the Toad is upon us.

Axatipe!

Rak Razam,
Venice Beach,
July 2015

PART ONE:

THE LITTLE TOAD
OF THE
SONORA DESERT

Otac: A First Look

The planet is alive and communicating with us through powerful chemical messengers. We can all hear it.

Thanks to advances in modern technology, knowledge of endoneurochemical processes, the newfound science of ethnobotany, and insights into the chemistry of plants and animals, we now know that the chemical reactions that happen in our brains are produced by a group of chemical messengers called neurotransmitters. These chemical messengers are related to a very select group of plants, considered sacred by some, and a gift from the gods. Also, in the realm of animals, there exists a magical and mythological toad called Otac (*Bufo alvarius*). The name originates from the Seri language, a native dialect of the desert state of Sonora, Mexico. From its glands, this toad produces natural chemical molecules capable of changing our perception of reality, replacing a senseless vision of life with one far more meaningful.

After many years of experimenting and studying sacred plants, I embarked on a journey to various natural places to witness rituals and experience the intake of natural sacraments in appropriate environments, in spite of prevalent information that demonizes these practices and the lack of relevant scientific reports. In all honesty, and perhaps only to confirm what I am now sharing, when I began to use salvia, peyote, LSD, MDMA, and psychoactive mushrooms, I crossed an invisible barrier that made a huge difference. A thin line separates a healthy psychoactive substance and one that isn't, substances that are harmful and those that are beneficial.

As you'll learn in Part Two: Full Disclosure, I had personally experienced the terrible confusion we are all exposed to, including the ready availability of cocaine and its popular variant, crack. I experienced cocaine for the first time when I was a teenager. Hard drugs like crystal meth, heroin, and cocaine have nothing to do with sacred entheogens. I know this now due to experience. Though very important to the Andean culture, due to the altitude in which it is found, the coca leaf, despite its being sacred to past civilizations, cannot be compared to ayahuasca, yopo, teonanácatl, hikuli, or Otac. The derivatives of the coca cause effects that can be devastating. The isolation of chemical substances, their concentrations, and the route of administration completely distorts the experience that nature arranged for proper contextualized use. Modernity and technology, combined with my own ignorance and inexperience, led to the enslavement of my spirit, the intoxication of my body, and the partial loss of my mind. I almost disappeared completely. For a couple of years, my life was a nightmare.

Thanks to the intervention of a close friend, Gerry, a doctor with whom I had shared my love for psychedelics at the beginning of my journey as a fledgling Man of Knowledge, I discovered Otac. After experimenting with *Salvia divinorum*, and subsequently with hikuli, I ultimately mixed the two entheogenic substances and had an experience that dramatically opened my consciousness to the existence of utterly unknown and unanticipated energies.

Using the quickest route of administration without violating the laws of nature (no injections!), I quickly understood with confidence that the molecules contained in the secretion of *Bufo alvarius* had a healing potential unlike anything I had ever known. These secretions are obtained by squeezing any of eight to ten glands of a living *Bufo*, located behind its eyes, arms, and legs. You simply press your fingers on the gland until the fluid is released and squirted onto a sheet of glass, then you free the toad. The dried fluid, when combusted and inhaled, becomes 5-MeO-DMT, the medicine. Since I learned firsthand of its efficacy, I have dedicated my free time to sharing this experience with whomever is qualified and interested.

Forging the Path to a New Reality

Many evolutionary processes had to occur for neurotransmitters, found alike in humans, plants, and animals all over the world, to reach the present state of concurrence. There is now evidence that effectively illustrates the close relationship between neurotransmitters and altered states of consciousness. Advances in molecular imaging and atomic structural analysis validates the importance of the chemical composition of our brains and, thus, our relationship with Otac and related plants.

Plants communicate with each other and with us through exogenous neurotransmitters found in their physical and organic compounds. Our bodies are designed to read the messages of neurotransmitters and so are able to decode the wisdom of neurotransmitter-rich plants, resulting in electrical reactions that translate as euphoric and dreamlike. More than that, extraordinary changes occur in the energetic polarity of each cell, penetrating the nucleus of the atoms themselves, which is a process that translates as health.

Mystical experiences induced by power plants, and more specifically by Otac, led me directly to experience this altered and alternative consciousness that I consider sacred. The power transmitted by nature leads us to a more precise understanding of inner peace, where tranquility and harmony reign in every moment.

During the nine years that I've been using the vapor of toad nectar, I've seen its effectiveness in the treatment of various affective and emotional disorders, as well as addictions. I have collected over three thousand testimonials reflecting the practical, medical, social, cultural, and spiritual benefits of this and other related substances.

The responses I have observed in patients have been highly favorable in comparison to any other therapy that I have seen. My experience in the treatment of addictions goes back to my job as director of various clinical and rehabilitation centers for addicts (including the BACC Foundation, Camp Rebirth in Guadalajara, and the Freedom Within Family Integration program in Jocotepec, Jalisco) as well as treating professionals from political/governmental and public safety, to the entertainment industry and more. I have also visited many self-help groups and conducted extensive reviews on incidences of abuse inside prisons.

I have spoken to people of every social class and age group, with and without a history of chronic degenerative illnesses. I have included people from twelve to ninety years old, pregnant women, people who'd experienced heart attacks, diabetes mellitus, hypertension, and intoxication due to all types substances — legal and illegal — schizophrenics, epileptics, people with renal disease, people with HIV, and so on. Asthma, bronchitis, depression, anxiety, insomnia, and traumas can be alleviated after a few sessions with this medicine. Longer still is the list of healthy individuals who have used toad medicine and discovered surprising benefits in their lives and health, inspiring general improvement in their interpersonal relationships.

If I'd had any doubts concerning the effectiveness and nobility of the substance, I would not have risked it. But I believe there is no actual contraindication; the substance already exists in the human body. However, the toad medicine is not for recreational use, and should be regulated. The experience you will soon be learning about should be undertaken in a controlled environment with guides who have training in natural medicines or the sacred power plants. These medicines are potent tools but in the wrong hands they can be dangerous. It is very important to emphasize that the environment in which one consumes hallucinogens is vital, maybe more important than the drug itself. Similarly, one's internal state is very influential in these types of experiences. The intention behind one's consumption is a third crucial factor. The reports of undesirable side effects have been dismantled with time and there is no data confirming that these substances are carcinogenic or teratogenic (able to disturb the growth or development of a fetus). As a matter of fact, the "model psychosis" induced by these psycho-integrative substances is highly therapeutic in many senses, as subjects can fully surrender to the knowledge offered by these experiences of life, light, and self-transformation. Creating the culture to respect, understand, and learn from these technologies will ensure safety.

If these constraints are in place, after experiencing the toad medicine the person returns to his or her life in a far better state, thinking, feeling and communicating better, more open and sincere. Overwhelmingly, this has been the case. After the experience, subjects are more functional and better able to prioritize their lives.

THE QUESTION REMAINS: HOW CAN THERE BE NEUROTRANSMITTERS IN PLANTS?

For healers of traditional shamanism, the answer to the above question is simple: these chemical neurotransmitters are the medium by which Gaia, i.e., the Earth, our collective mother, communicates with all of us. These days, that may be less obvious due to the homogenization of communication media and the advent of the Internet.

The main findings that confirm the relationship between the mystical and entheogens are archaeological, with plenty of support from worldwide myth. There are numerous excavations in the oldest settlements around the world that demonstrate a longstanding relationship between shamanic magic and altered states of consciousness induced by the ecstasy of sacred plants. These altered states of consciousness were accompanied by various rituals of celebratory song and dance, colorful costumes, and ornaments of all kinds. The result was a beautiful festival of life and the creativity of Spirit.

The oldest forms of celebration have a close relationship with the ceremonial use of sacred plants and animals. In Mesoamerica, for example, the Otac toad is represented as a being connected to the "other reality," accompanied by the most important figures of ancient cosmogony around the planet. Amphibians have frequently been depicted in ancient mythology as representing magic and religion. Due to the scant and often erroneous information on the matter, there is a strong need to reinterpret "history."

A LOOK INTO THE PAST

The time has come for humankind to explore its origins, and not just to obsess over mythology or to create new religions. We need to analyze and understand the way in which past civilizations managed social balance and even transcended time. The answers have always been right in front of us. Discovering the obvious, we learn, requires not so much the physical senses as the mental.

The balance of mind, body, and soul is accessible only through the same substances our organism produces naturally. We should remember that said substances found in nature are just as ancient as those found in our brains, as they are the same. Who first had these components, animals or plants? What is their actual function? And why is it that the intolerance and denial of their magical properties only continues to provoke more curiosity?

We do not know with certainty the processes that caused the origin and development of life up to this moment. Yet, surprisingly, the key to life is found everywhere. The deciphering process is left to our centers of perception. We need to focus our internal lens to be able to visualize exactly what we do not see at the beginning. It is believed that our distant ancestors went from plant to lower animal, then took a quantum leap to hominid. The most logical thing to assume is that these transformations began with the introduction of different foods into their diets, each of these diets a teacher. This is how Mother Nature communicates with her children.

With time, our ancestors began to manage fire; only then was there light during the night. No more cold and darkness. Then we began to investigate various foods and the alchemy of cooking. Then came medicines like ayahuasca and the toad of the Sonora Desert, Otac, *Bufo alvarius*, the toad of the dawn. The experiences provided by plants that contain DMT and another exogenous neurotransmitters were part of the daily life of prehumans. Such teachers are the last vestige of a renewable natural resource with the potential to change our world and history, to get us back on the right path. Study ancient history and you'll find a remarkable similarity among the stories and mythologies in ancient Asia, Europe, and Mesoamerica.

The use of magical mushrooms has been extensively studied in recent years. Well known is Albert Hofmann's visit to Mexico in search of teonanácatl and *Salvia divinorum*. Hofmann, alongside R. Gordon Wasson and others, visited the Mazatec Sierra to meet Maria Sabina. Years later they would return to the Sierra with a synthesized chemical of the molecule. As the story goes, the famous Mazatec shaman took the psilocybin pills and, after ingesting them, remarked that she did not feel any effects from the "holy children fabricated by the white man" and discredited modern science saying that "while the effects were similar, in comparison to those fabricated by men, the holy mushrooms are superior in their magic as they contain the spirit of the plant."

Maria Sabina emphasized the importance of respecting not only the molecules found in nature, but nature itself. She insisted that beliefs in the supernatural did not interfere with truthful experience. Quite the contrary, such beliefs are part of the wealth of knowledge flowing from ancient peoples. She valued the use of these plants in modern life but advised never to believe we can outdo nature in its wisdom.

Therefore we must realize that all substances considered to be hallucinogenic have a specific function for the body, since that is what the chemical receptors in the brain have shown. It's no coincidence that these natural chemical compounds can cross the blood-brain barrier, activate intricate processes in the neurological and nervous systems, and produce highly meaningful experiences. This explains why these plants were used as sacred medicine by so many ancient cultures, which have left behind evidence of their surrender to nature. In this way, man and plant together enter sacred ground and become part of many spiritual practices. In addition, through my own personal experimentation and the knowledge acquired through those of others, I can confirm the existence of the mystical state as a real one. Very real, too, is the communication of nature's wisdom through the intake of hormonal and cerebral neurotransmitters found in certain living things. This has been proven by analysis of the combustion fumes of the desiccated nectar found in the parotid glands of Otac.

The incredible thing about this toad, as well as power plants, is that they have the correct concentrations and necessary enzymes for the methylation (the addition of a methyl group to a molecule) of O-Methyl-bufotenin into 5-MeO-DMT for a rapid and easy absorption. This particular set of molecules is easy to manipulate to create special states of consciousness. In the right doses, they open new dimensional portals in our lives and heal our species. They induce deep meditational states that connect and correct human consciousness.

The function exerted by the chemical substances that provoke these visions, altered states of consciousness, mysticism, and the evolution of thought around the globe, are unknown to modern science and remain unclear to almost all of modern society. Also unknown is the reason behind human existence because we have buried almost all traces of the original use of these substances and the resultant understandings. But there is hope for the human worldview with the reemergence of shamanic practices involving natural medicines, supported by archeological evidence and the study of traditional medicines.

OTAC: UP CLOSE

The cult of the toad existed in pre-Christian Europe, where women owned metal relics relating the toad to the uterus. And all over the world in art, mythology, and popular culture, the toad has been part of pagan rituals and often asociated with witchcraft.

The Sonora Desert has an area of two hundred thousand square kilometers, extending from California and Arizona in the US to Sonora, Mexico. The desert rises to 1,700 meters above sea level. Arid lands are covered by huizache and mesquite trees. It rains only a few centimeters each year, and temperatures can reach 113° F/45° C during summer, and sometimes up to 122 F/50° C. It is a desert with a variety of animals and plants that make it unique in the world. There is archeological proof that a thousand years

ago, native Hookaams made changes in channels of rivers, contributing to an increase of the territory of *Bufo alvarius*, also called Colorado River toad or bull toad.

Of 463 total toad species, *Bufo alvarius* is the only one whose glands contain the neurotransmitting molecule bufotenin, 5-MeO-DMT (or 5-methoxy-N-N-dimethyltryptamine) and the enzyme capable of methylating it — unique properties in a very singular animal. Despite the Bufonidae family being distributed almost throughout the world (all except for Australia, New Guinea, and the Polar Artic), it should be noted that this species is endemic only to the Sonora Desert. It does not exist in any other part of the world. These toads are nocturnal and only emerge to the surface during July and August. Like other tailless amphibians (frogs), Otac does not have teeth. Its pupils are horizontal. This is a jumping quadruped with strong limbs.

It is quite flexible and agile. Its skin is thick and wrinkly. The difference between this and other toads lies in the molecular components of substances sheltered in the parotid gland, which serve both as a defense and as an attractant to its prey. These toads have no natural predators and are completely harmless to humans and other large animal species. The toad comes out from underground only after it rains. When the first drops of water touch the ground they emerge from underground to celebrate by singing and copulating. They eat many kinds of insects, eggs, small rodents, and other frogs; hence the mythological belief that sees this toad as a dualistic mother, symbolizing the earth in the give-and-take of life.

The differences between *Bufo alvarius* and other Sonoran toads such as *Bufo californicus*, *Bufo retiformis* and *Bufo debilis* are size, color, population, geographical distribution, and life cycle, making it unmistakable among others. Unlike *Bufo alvarius*, which contains bufotenin, there are toads that are dangerous and their venom contains various amounts of bufotoxin, a poisonous substance. In fact, in the Amazon River basin, there is a tree frog that measures less than an inch but has enough poison to kill over a thousand mice. When the species *Bufo alvarius* feels threatened, they will inflate their bodies. Males are usually smaller than females and their genitals are internal, which hinders sex identification.

Although there are rumors online about dried toad skin being sold by certain dealers, in truth this species is protected in Mexico by the indigenous tribes of Sonora, the government, and the Otac Foundation. Together, they control the uses of this toad, which is seen as ancient medicine. The intention is to bring awareness to the importance of the preservation and care of such a valuable species, and the toad's nectar must be collected without harming the animal.

To standardize the dose, it is important to begin with the greatest possible number of specimens, the concentration of the active ingredients being different depending on age and size. It is also necessary to differentiate between the bufotenin found in the Otac and the bufotoxin found in other creatures. This is the main difference that makes the Otac so special.

Consumption of Bufotoxin

This substance is said to cause serious problems in dogs and cats. Symptoms, appearing just minutes after consuming the poison, include irritation followed by a hypersensitivity that can include cardiac abnormalities. Other symptoms are itchiness, depression, weakness, lung collapse, cardiac arrest, and convulsions. They can also include dizziness, diarrhea, and vomiting. If adequate treatment isn't given, cardiovascular symptoms may prove fatal in dogs or cats that ingest the toxin.

It is important to distinguish between bufotoxin and bufotenin, and it must be noted that bufotenin becomes 5-MeO-DMT when methylized.

In my fieldwork, I have seen dogs and cats coexisting with Otac, so personally I dismiss reports of deaths in domestic animals through contact with the *Bufo alvarius* toad.

Otac and Psychoactive Plants
in a Historical Context

We know of about four hundred psychoactive plants in the world. All of them have been used since ancient times for medicinal and divinatory purposes in every culture of the world. One could say that Mexico, in this way, is the true Promised Land, for it contains sacred plants like no other part of the world. Their concentration, distribution, and variety makes Mexico a paradise of psycho-integraters. The country is almost completely surrounded by water without being an island, it has every type of climate, it possesses unique micro environments with exquisite proliferations of nature despite centuries of over-exploitation. Mexico continues to be home to hundreds of thousands of starving poor and as many wasteful gluttons, both Mexican and foreign.

Living beings such as cannabis, *Salvia divinorum*, mescaline cacti (peyote), psychedelic mushrooms, Sonora toad, ayahuasca, olioliuqui seeds, and the African iboga, have lives and properties of their own. This includes Albert Hofmann's and Alexander Shulguin's creations (drugs such as LSD, MDMA, ketamine, 2CB) based on molecular structures that have active principles causing mental illusion. All of these can take us to mystical states and states of self-transformation. Recently renamed psycho-integrators (a more actual and appropriate term than *hallucinogens*), these are a very select group of chemical substances found naturally in some plants and animals that have a unique effect on the mind and its capacity to perceive reality.

There is confusion in our languages, and general ignorance on the subject, so let's quickly go over some of the varieties of psychoactive plants and their uses. The relationship between our culture and these living things is complex and encompasses chemistry, mental disposition, and social and historic context in the fields of psychopharmacology, ethnobotany, biochemistry, history, archeology, medicine, and philosophy.

Comparing the techniques of nonchemical ecstasy to those involving traditional plants used by ancients, we may sometimes find ourselves trying to reinvent the wheel. Many people are awaiting the discovery of "new" hallucinogenic substances due to the disappearance of historical records, of which many were orally communicated, and the "forgetfulness" of participants who wished to hide from the prying eyes of strangers. The researcher's task is to scientifically rediscover, redescribe, and reexperience these living substances with the intention of a useful modern interpretation. The challenges of such work are exciting and the enterprise completely legitimate because alternate states of consciousness are a longstanding part of the human experience, with much historical and archeological evidence.

In Mexico, the use of plants and substances that alter consciousness goes back to the beginning of time. There are many varieties of endemic psychoactive medicinal plants, including: the sacred mushroom (psilocybin), the hikuli (*Lopophora williamsii*), the pastor leaves (*Salvia divinorum*), seeds of the Virgin (*Ipomoea violacea*) and, though not a plant, the sacred toad Otac (*Bufo alvarius*). Reports of the first Spanish conquistadores speak of approximately eighty psychoactive plants plus medicinal plants amounting to over a thousand. These reports do not reflect the number of plants recognized as useful in the ancient world of Mesoamerica, but they give us an idea.

The global prohibition of mind-altering substances is recent. In the United States it began in 1937. In Mexico, a law was enacted in 1871 to restrict the use of such intoxicants. Mexico considered a bill in 1917 that would ban alcohol, different varieties of pulque, and gambling, cockfighting, horse racing, and bullfighting — but the bill was rejected. Later, in 1925, the government legalized some intoxicants, but hallucinogens were not among them.

Let us not forget the revolution in consciousness expansion in the United States in the 1960s. This followed the discovery of LSD, which added to popular knowledge of ethnobotany, aided by the work of Richard Evans Schultes and Albert Hofmann. In truth, most of us use some type of chemical, natural, or synthetic drug many times a day, whether legal or illegal: refined sugar and industrialized foods are examples, and there are many other types of self-intoxication similarly used to produce pleasure at whatever cost (think of our current profligate consumption of material goods and entertainment for escape, social recognition, sexual arousal, and ego fulfillment — plus other things I would rather not describe).

Anthropologists have long speculated that people of ancient Mesoamerica used *Bufo marinus*, a principal inhabitant of the coast of the Gulf of Mexico, in an inebriating ritual. This hypothesis is based on the many iconographic and mythological representations of frogs, plus many ethnographic reports. However, many authors reject the *Bufo marinus* as a candidate for such a claim because its venom is highly toxic. The only viable candidate is *Bufo alvarius*. In *Bufo alvarius*, the fluid becomes lethal only if ingested orally in a dose of 400 mg/kg. That is, a person of 176 lbs./80 kg. could safely eat about 32 grams/1.13 oz. of bufotenin. However, this amount inhaled as a gas would be sufficient to provide an experience to over two hundred people, so it would be a waste. In its gaseous state, there is no way to overdose with the substance. Therefore, it cannot be termed a poison, as it is nontoxic when smoked, the safest method of administration.

Bufo marinus was discarded as the representative entity in the Mayan effigies worshipped in the ancient Olmec sites due to its toxicity levels, as illustrated by the figures found in the Cuajilote zone in Veracruz where, next to an enormous sweat lodge, there is an effigy of a toad that emphasizes its secreting gland, with three "Sun Circles," symbol of the cosmic energy. Bufotenin, 5-MeO-DMT, and NN-DMT are produced inside the human body, all mammal brains, and some plants. This is why they are also called organic entheogens, endo-psycho-amines, and natural neurotransmitters. In other words, they are cerebral hormones.

Moreover, the substance within *Bufo alvarius* has more than 15% 5-MeO-DMT. The toad is the only animal producer of entheogens worldwide. There are no hypotheses, theories, nor reasonable speculations about why this toad contains this precious substance in its glands. There is no clear evidence to prove its use by pre-Columbian peoples. However, due to the large number of psychoactive plants in the territory, it is assumed that the Sonora toad was revered as a deity due to its complex neuro-enzyme activity. That is also why it is common to see images of toads in Mayan burials.

The main compound secreted by the parotid glands in *Bufo alvarius* is 5-MeO-DMT (5-metoxi-N, N-dimethyltryptamine). This substance is a neurotransmitter and belongs to the psycho-integrator group of tryptamines. Besides bufotenin (5-hydroxy-DMT), there is DMT (N, N-DMT), a component of numerous varieties of fungi used for thousands of years by shamans as an entheogen for part of their religious rituals. DMT was isolated from yopo tree seeds in 1959 and from *Bufo alvarius* in 1968. It is a compound also present in ayahuasca. There is no recent history of use by indigenous communities in Mexico's national territory. Only archeological and historical data places Otac as an element in the ancient cultures of Mesoamerica.

Ancient healing techniques applied by the Kunkaks use 5-MeO-DMT and other amines of said nectar to produce profound physical biochemical effects in the organisms of those who volunteer for such a process.

Below is a chronological list of the most significant events in the field of psycho-integration:

— 1912. The Merck amphetamine laboratory did work leading to the future development of Ecstasy and crystal meth.

— 1937. DMT (dimethyltryptamine) was first synthesized
by Richard Manske during the great wave of chemical
experimentation following the discovery of mescaline
in the late nineteenth century. DMT was isolated inde-
pendently from three different plant sources, *Mimosa
hostilis* (*M. tenuiflora*) in 1946, *Piptadenia macrocarpa*
(*Anadenanthera colubrina*, a variety of Cebil) and
Piptadenia peregrina (*Anadenanthera peregrina*) in 1955.

— 1938. LSD-25. This discovery was made by Albert
Hofmann in Basel, Switzerland, in the Sandoz Laboratory.
The discovery of the divine mushroom cult by Robert
Gordon Wasson, as well as his tenure with indigenous
people of Mexico, was made that same year. Subsequent
investigations happened throughout the mid 1950s,
centered around a cult that survived the Spanish
Inquisition and was relegated to the most inhospitable
places in the high mountains of the southern states
of Mexico.

— 1941. The Olioliuqui seed, *Rivea corymbosa*, was discovered, which contains the active component LSA (lysergic
acid amide). Twenty years later, it would be linked to the
active ingredient in LSD (lysergic acid diethylamide).

— 1951 – 1960. Excavation of Shanidar Cave in Iraq
revealed the body of a Neanderthal buried sixty thousand

years ago along with ten psychoactive plants. Ralph Solecki, archeologist in charge, demonstrated not only the antiquity of the knowledge of psychoactive botany but also their importance. This was one of the biggest scientific contributions that support the hypothesis presented here.

— 1956. Psychedelic DMT effects were described by Stephen Szara. It became illegal in 1966 due to the writings of Ralph Metzner, Timothy Leary, and William Burroughs.

— 1965. 5-MeO-DMT is found in the secretion of the glands of *Bufo alvarius.*

DMT, forgotten for decades, reappeared when Rick Strassman took it in a study approved by the FDA, done at the beginning of the 1990s and described in the 2000 book *DMT: The Spirit Molecule.*

The 5-MeO-DMT was first synthesized in 1936, but its expansive properties of the mind were not recognized until 1959, when scientists isolated their psychoactive components in a family tree of Rue evergreen shrubs, *Dictyoloma incanesce.* In 1937, it was isolated from *Anadenanthera peregrina*, giving evidence that it is the main component of Yoperos of South America. (These people in their infinite knowledge made consciousness-altering powders using plants, seeds, flowers, and leaves of native plants. Curiously, this substance is found naturally in mammalian brains.)

Remains were found that showed ritual use of 5-MeO-DMT for medicinal purposes in the Chavin culture, which blossomed in the Atacama Desert in Chile more than 4,500 years ago, linking Tiahuanaco with Otac.

— 1966. Claudio Naranjo published results of the application of ibogaine, a plant-derived psychedelic, in psychiatric treatments.

— 1968. Robert Gordon Wasson related the soma of the Vedas of India to the mushroom *Amanita muscaria*. That same year, *Bufo alvarius* was identified as the bearer of neurotransmitters 5-MeO-DMT and bufotenin.

— 2012. "Otac, the Story" began. I realized that sacred medicines have always existed and have been of use to humanity in all continents throughout time.

In more recent times, researchers firmly established the close relationship between the active ingredients in various ancient sacred medicines and the biological components naturally active in the brain, and the importance of the transmission of signals in our body. For example, serotonin

(5-hydroxytryptamine, or 5-HT) and its close affinity and relationship with DMT, 5-MeO-DMT, psilocybin, ASD, LSD, and ibogaine was discovered; the relationship between mescaline and norepinephrine was proven; and norepinephrine was linked to caffeic acid.

Another important moment came when ethnobotanist Richard Evans Schultes and anthropologist Raoul Weston La Barre located the psychedelic phenomenon in the historical and ideological cultural framework. It was established as going back to the Paleolithic period. This was one of the more memorable moments in the rediscovery of these magical substances.

Historical Native American interest in plants had nothing to do with survival, thus the emphasis was not botanical but cultural. This is one of the greatest distinctions in culture and worldview between the indigenous American and the indigenous European. It is assumed that this difference stems from Paleo-Mesolithic Eurasian shamanism in which hunters of large animals from Northeast Asia came to America across the Bering Strait during the last ice age, about twenty thousand years ago. We know of the relationship between mysticism and the intoxication of the senses with certain magical potions, sacred foods, and special activities. It is impossible to deny the close connection between the magical state and the necessity to provide pleasure and satisfaction to our mental base as a survival mechanism.

It is very important to highlight the fact that there are many mushroom stones found in various archeological sites, numbering in the hundreds. They are related to the toad stones and are graphic and artistic representations of the olioliuqui (*Rivea corymbosa*). In the desert of Tassili, in Algeria, there are caves filled with parietal art that represent the earliest forms of human artistic creation. In these caves, there are repetitive elements that form a pattern showing with clarity very different forms of animals, human beings, and beings that do not correspond to our nature. There are even sacred mushrooms. These hieroglyphics look a lot like the ones found in different parts of the world. In other words, there are images of supernatural beings everywhere, and they have existed along with world mythology as a product, no doubt, of visions induced by ingesting sacred plants in collective ritualistic ways for healing and worship. For example, the mythical teonanácatl, flesh of the Aztec god, has been identified as Mexican Psilocybes. And psilocybin, the active ingredient in the famous fungus named by Albert Hofmann, was closely linked in molecular structure to serotonin, one of the main cerebral neurotransmitters.

Drugs and Medicines

To better understand the effects of psychoactive drugs, let's begin with the three basic types: stimulants, depressants (or narcotic sedatives), and psycho-integrators (hallucinogens).

The stimulants include coffee, tea, cocaine, amphetamines, and methamphetamines.

The second group, the depressants, includes opium, morphine, and alcohol.

In the third group, the psycho-integrators, we find all the sacred plants, for which we have terms that in no way adequately describe their characteristics, nor define their fascinating properties. These terms include: hallucinogenic, illusionegenic, psychedelic, entheogenic, mysticometic, onirogenic, fanerotimes, psycholdelic, fantastical, psycho-metric, psychogenic, psychotoxic, schyzotoxic, and deliriant, among others.

Of the three groups, the one that helps us most in the current discussion is the psycho-integrators (hallucino-gens), divided into tryptamines and phenylethylamines. Tryptamines are compounds that affect the relaxation and contraction of blood vessels, and thus blood pressure. They are derived from tryptophan (just two molecular steps away). Tryptamines are very simple and widespread, found practically everywhere, in plants, animals, and humans. Indoles are crystalline alkoid compounds that can be made synthetically, and are decomposition products of proteins containing tryptophan. The tryptamines are subcategorized as either flexible (natural) or rigid (semi-synthetic, such as LSD). DMT, psilocybin and LSD and iboga, are some examples of the tryptamine compounds, while mescaline and peyote and the Cactus of St. Peter are natural phenylethylamines.

All others are semi-synthetic and were developed by Alex Shulguin. At least 130 compounds were investigated by Shulguin. Salvinorin A and high-level THC are examples of hallucinogens called diptamines, since they don't have nitrogen; in other words, they are alkaline.

Your Body is the True Laboratory

Our brains are completely filled with molecular receptors for different organic chemical compounds capable of altering our states of being. Meaning, our emotions are chemical and electrical impulses produced by these substances in the body, which are influenced by a group of plants and one very special amphibian. The development of the pharmaceutical industry and various scientific discoveries have taken us to a revolution of knowledge that, without a doubt, will change the world and the way we lead our lives in the future.

The following table shows how, for each psychoactive substance, there is an equivalent in our brains. The cerebral receptors specifically show a close bond with each of these molecules found in nature.

Analogies Between Exogenous and Endogenous Neurotransmitters

EXOGENOUS NEUROTRANSMITTER	ENDOGENOUS NEUROTRANSMITTER
TRYPTAMINES/INDOLES	
Bufotenin	Bufotenin
5-MeO-DMT	5-MeO-DMT
Harmaline/harmine	B-carbolines: (harmane)
Ibogaine	B-carbolines
Lysergic acid derivatives	Endopsychedelics
N,N-DMT	N,N-DMT

EXOGENOUS NEUROTRANSMITTER	ENDOGENOUS NEUROTRANSMITTER
Psilocybin/psilocin	Serotonin
Strychnine	Glycine
Yohimbine	B-carbolines

PHENETHYLAMINES

Amphetamine and derivatives (MDMA, ephedrine)	Adrenaline
B-phenethylamine	B-phenethylamine
Cocaine	Noradrenaline
Mescaline	Dopamine

MORPHINE AND OPIUM ALKALOIDS

Codeine	Codeine
Morphine	Morphine
Opiates/heroin	Endorphins/encephalins

TROPANE ALKALOIDS

Atropine	Acetylcholine
Hyoscyamine	Acetylcholine
Scopolamine	Acetylcholine

VARIOUS GROUPS

Diazepam (Valium)	Endovalium
Ibotenic acid	Glutamate
Muscimol	GABA
Nicotine	Acetylcholine
PCP/ketamine	Angeldustine
THC/cannabinoids	Anandamide

Table extracted from *The Encyclopedia of Psychoactive Plants* by Christian Ratsch (Rochester, VT: Park Street Press, 1998), p. 811. (From Perrine* 1996, Snyder* 1989 Zehentbahuer* 1992; supplemented)

OTAC IN HISTORY AND ART

A few months after I began this book, the Toad Project began, where I was seeking the support of government agencies and making sure to notify relevant health authorities to not infringe on my applications of these healing therapies. My brother, David, who has a doctorate in archeology and graduated from the National School of Anthropology and History, was living in Germany. Via Internet I asked for his help accessing information from scientific journals regarding Mayan toads and specifically *Bufo alvarius*.

Among the first articles I received was one with geographical specifications of the Sonoran Desert, including climate and a list of endemic animals and plants. Another that caught my attention was that of an archaeologist named Hobkins who talked about three figures repeated very often in ceremonial burials of classic Mayan culture, which were the mushroom stones, representations of the olioliuqui flower, and stone toads. Another article referred to the mystery surrounding mythological and sacred archeology of the region.

I learned there are many theories as to the constant veneration by ancient cultures toward *Bufo alvarius*. Certainly the ancients referred many times to an important toad. As I've mentioned, at first it was thought to be *Bufus marinus*, but its high toxicity ruled out *marinus* as a possible candidate. Thanks to the Internet and the information available in Maya codices, steles, and stone figures around the world, and with the help of archaeologists José Francisco Hinojosa and David Rettig Hinojosa, better information finally began to emerge.

It is known that Tlaltecutli was the Goddess Earth Mother toad of the Aztecs, as is pictured in Andean art. In Japan, Finland, and China, the mystical properties of this amphibian are also known, but no one has been able to explain its specific role. Only *Bufo alvarius*, after pyrolysis (thermochemical decomposition in the presence of high heat) of the nectar found in its glands, produces the states described in various legends. Thus mythology then becomes science.

I must emphasize that the places sacred medicine can take you to are inaccessible in any other way. In its natural form, toad medicine is not only the most potent entheogen but also the only known one of its kind. It is the missing link of pre-Columbian ethnopharmacology and the missing piece of the Mayan's toad-mushroom–magic flower trilogy discovered by Hobkins in 1974. Aztecs, Olmecs, and subsequent cultures knew and used these substances. Let us remember that *Bufo alvarius* is the only specimen of over 463 types of toad that contains this powerful tryptamine agent. *Bufo alvarius* is also the only amphibian capable of storing so many neurotransmitters that are easily metabolized by our bodies through the respiratory tract.

Bufo alvarius is the only key that opens the door leading to knowledge of the mystical state described by ancient Incan mythology as the land of Pachamama. Upon analyzing the figures found in the Frieze of the Four Kings in the Mayan ruins in Balamku, Campeche, we clearly see four Otacs (Xpek was the original name in Quiché or modern Mayan). There are also four human figures in a meditational/submissive position with the same elements that appear consistently as effigies of *Bufo alvarius*, their glands like visionary rings and spirals, symbols of transformation and the Olioliuqui vine. These beings emerge from the jaws of the toad dressed allegorically as though participating in an entheogenic festivity. We can only imagine what actually happened, due to the subsequent destruction of practically all written records of the time.

Detail of señor on
a frog

This is the toad
with its jaws open,
supported by
a cushion.

Nose

Upper lip

Eye

Corner
of the
mouth

Lower
lip

In the image below, sacred mushrooms and hikuli, aside
from other psychoactive plants such as the Sinicuichi, are
found surrounding Otac. Specific reference is made to its
glands, as in other toad effigies shown in this volume.
We can also see the eye of vision, the knots of wisdom,
and a meditative posture. (Taken from a fresco in Tulum,
Quintana Roo.)

Below, is a photo of the Cuajilote toad in Veracruz. This is a very large and very important archeological site, a square for ten thousand people, temazcal ("sweat lodge"), and juego de pelota ("ballgame") with fifteen hundred objects related to the celebration of fertility and reproduction.

Cuajilote toad sculpture, front, back, and gland pattern as the sun disc.

The great ball court next to the sweat lodge where the sculptures of the toad are found is yet another indicator that the proliferation of closed architectonic structures was not only for the purpose of sweating. There were more important reasons. The breathing in of the enclosed vapors, rich in tryptamine acids, created electrochemical reactions within the nervous system, as my research data clearly demonstrates. And it is not only physical research but the historical touchstones that make this interpretation so compelling.

Ballgame goal, with the toad image, exhibited in National Anthropology Museum of Mexico City.

The following image shows one of many toad stones found together with a mushroom stone in a Mayan excavation.

In the following photograph, on the bowl is an Otac kneeling like nobility, inlaid with jewels, on its glands a type of collar, with beings that refer to the suctioning of the nectar that comes directly from the Earth and ascends up to the upper parotid gland. Along with the toad, we have the deer, a sacred ruminant for the Mesoamericans, which is necessary for the hatching cycle of the psilocybin fungi. These are also represented on the previous image, coming from the same place as the figures of the Otac medicine, from the bark of Mother Earth. In the strip that connects the space between earth and the sky, there is the feathered serpent Quetzalcoatl of Kukulkan, who presents reality as a thin, fragile fabric such as a theater curtain.

Photograph by Justin Kerr.

The pictured Olmec vase was for the combustion or methylation of nectar.

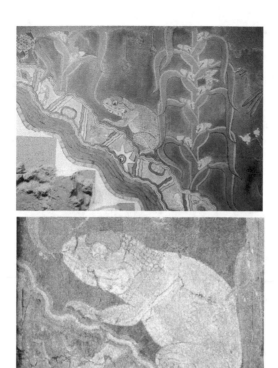

Mural of Cacaxtla, Tlaxcala.

In the image below, we see a Mayan artifact that describes
the *Bufo alvarius* (not the *marinus*) and proof of the
inhaling of the secretion of its glands by the Mayans. The
toad has the indicative diamond pattern with dots over the
gland, the classic "cross" on the back, the three dots on the
head, the frontal lobe flower, and he is offering in a turtle
shell an eye and a hand—he is offering the new vision.

The rest of the vase depicts how Quetzalcoatl guides or leads the shaman to inhale the substance from a shell with the three dots, who afterward transforms into the jaguar. The jaguar is the classic symbol of the shaman-warrior on an altered state of the mind and soul, in which the "underworld" is explored to understand the knowledge that nature teaches.

Photo by Leonardo Bondani

Next we look at the Dresden Codex, named after the city in Germany where the artifact is exhibited today. This is one of the few original Mayan documents that remain to the present day. It clearly illustrates the mythology behind the toad and sacred plants. There are effigies of magical mushrooms eaten by a fish that turns into a toad. Also seen is the state of consciousness before, during, then after the experience of absorbing through their airways the product of methylation found in the *Bufo*. They do not eat the toad itself, as we see represented in different ways.

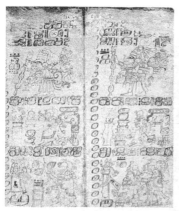

It is a clear codification of the transcendent gifts of the beings of power, and specifically *Bufo alvarius*, as the only known animal capable of producing said states of consciousness.

Below are two stone tablets found in Izapa. They, too, testify to the mystical properties of *Bufo alvarius*.

Understanding Reality Through
the Lens of Religion

Now let's talk about the different religious doctrines of our
time, which are based on archaic moral precepts that, in
the vast majority, were inspired by dreams, altered states of
reality, trances, visions, apparitions, or divine messages of
every stripe. To the detractors of entheogenic spirituality,
we say that in ancient times before the dominion of institutional religions, all primal religions, including Christianity
in the West, plus every other European, Mediterranean,
Asian, African, etc., religion used ecstatic trance as a way
of reaching a mystical experience which is, when it comes
down to it, what we are all seeking.

Meaning, the contemporary use of psycho-integrative
substances can be seen as a form of neo-religion and a resurgence of primal faith in response to our need for actual feelings
of belonging and safety. For the first time in the history of our
race, we have the capacity to obtain a varied supply of spiritual
medicines that expand our mind and consciousness and offer
us the opportunity for direct spiritual experience.

The most ancient religions and their belief in a higher
being or beings go hand in hand with substances that alter
the mind and expand the consciousness. Three thousand
years ago, Hindu Vedas referred to an entheogen, used to

inspire sacred texts, called soma. All images obtained from exhaustive research illustrate that soma is the mystical mushroom, *Amanita muscaria*. The sacred mushroom contains psilocybin, a molecule closely linked to the 5-OH-DMT bufotenin, a neurotransmitter found in all mammals, mostly in primates and even more so in humans. It is believed that the neurotransmitters found in these sacred plants are closely related to the development of the consciousness of our species. They also serve as a unique source of creativity, inspiration, and wellbeing, mentally and spiritually. Shamanism also serves as medicine for healing the body.

Kykeon was used for two thousand years in the Eleusinian Mysteries, considered to be the pinnacle of Greek civilization. The Mazatec have teonanácatl and Venezuelans have yagé. For the Amazonians, it is the epena. In Africa there is the tabernathe iboga, in Australia there is wikla, in Thailand krakoom, and Antilleans have yopo.

In the Far East, Taoists would use mushrooms and mineral substances in the same way to induce a religious trance. In Siberia and the North of Europe, *Amanita muscaria* is still used by shamans for healing and divine purposes.

Cactus trichocereus, which contains mescaline, has been used by the Chavin culture of Peru for more than three thousand years. It is called St. Peter's Cactus precisely because it holds the key to heaven.

The cult of hikuli (*Lophophora williamsii*) practiced by Indians of the Native American Church, the Mexican Huicholes, Tarahumaras, Seris, and other surviving cultures, has continued despite the opposition of the institutional church. These substances have been used for divinatory and mystical purposes since the beginning of history. These plants, containing tryptamine, have also long been used in the Caribbean and the Antilles, just as cannabis, tobacco, *Salvia divinorum*, the seeds of the morning glory plant, and psilocybin.

The seeds of the Cebil tree (*Anadenanthera peregrina*) are also known as Cohoba, and from this the name of Cuba is derived. These seeds form a central role in old ritual practices of South America and the Antilles. Its main active ingredient is 5-MeO-DMT. The Epena, or Virola, tree has the same active ingredient. Gordon Wasson remained convinced that *Amanita muscaria* was behind the mystery of soma, which is still in use by Siberian tribes with their shamanic cults.

Given the number of interpretative mistakes made by science in the past, it is necessary to say quite precisely that when you hear of "feeding the gods," we are talking about taking sacred plants, not offering the gods blood nor any other human sacrifice. Giving gratitude is our offering, which has always been part of magical, mystical, and ecstatic experimentation with power plants.

Inhaling the Sacrament

For consumption of the toad medicine, all you need is
a glass pipe and a source of fire. It's that simple. While
some claim that using a vaporizer has its advantages, I
find it wastes the toad medicine, and that a torch lighter
works best. You can also take it in a closed room like a
sweat lodge.

Before initiating the process of heating the molecules in the
glass pipe, it should be emphasized that deep breaths must
be taken, followed by complete exhalations so all of it is
absorbed, or the smoke will condense on the glass and lose
potency very quickly.

Once you are relaxed, you must stand up and breathe many
times through your nose and exhale through your mouth to
reconnect with the rhythm of your breath.

Then, the person guiding you through the experience places
the 5-MeO-DMT into the glass receptacle and the lighter is
lit. The intensity of the flame is most important, as it must
be very high. When the substance begins to crack and snap
due to the heat, it will release a bright amber- and white-
colored smoke. Inhaling has to be done firmly, softly, and
with will and desire. You breathe in the medicine (vapors)
through your mouth, filling up all of your lungs, and hold

the medicine as long as you can. There must be complete surrender and purpose. We must know what we're looking for and hoping to find. We are just a breath away.

After you've inhaled the vapors, what you see isn't that important. Your visions won't be as colorful as those triggered by other tryptamines, as the colors and fractals are so fast. What's most significant is the feeling you experience, a melding with the universe, a feeling of oneness. You experience a dissolution of your "self." Breathing is very important, breathing is connected to what you feel. Letting go is as important as taking in. You need to surrender. There is no preparation for receiving your experience.

With the majority of psycho-integrators, the person becomes very susceptible to emotion. There may be childhood traumas, frustrated desires, repressed memories, or dreams impossible to achieve in a state of "normalcy." The surrounding environment is also an important factor, as environmental odors and fragrances influence the personal experience. It is best to choose a place that is calm, peaceful, private, safe, and quiet (silent or with calm music), with sweet aromas (incense, copal, sacred herb stick) and the company of nice people, perhaps in the intimacy of your own home. If you are consuming a higher dosage of the medicine, it is best to do so outside.

It is important to have clean thoughts and emotions at the time of taking a natural psycho-integrative medicine. We must consider the precedent of the cultures where it was used with intention and ritual. We must understand that the shaman does not have any special powers and that the true master is in the medicinal molecules and their animating spirit. We must have the wisdom to minimize contamination of the experience by the person who administers the medicine. In a state of trance, more than allowing us to see the future, the medicine helps us create it.

THE CORRECT DOSAGE

It is important to note that experiences vary with individuals, their reasons for doing it, and the circumstances surrounding them. It is common to hear people say that "it was like eternity in this place, with no time or space." Some people remember white light for only a fraction of a second when, in reality, fifteen or twenty minutes will have gone by.

Finding the right dose for each person is very important, due to the potency of the substance. It is recommended to begin with the lowest dose possible. In the case of toad medicine, that would be about twenty milligrams, increasing until a maximum of 120 milligrams. Adequate dosage is important so that the person will remember the experience. However, variables in the individual's reaction to environmental stimuli are also important parameters. The best gauge to measure the effectiveness of the dose and experience is not done by the patient him- or herself but by the family. Dosage must be adjusted individually, always remembering the basic adage to use the minimum dose required. Contrary to popular belief, the proper dosage for 5-MeO-DMT has no relationship to body weight. Meaning those who are bigger do not need more. The dose must be sufficient but not too much, as negative side effects such as nausea, vomiting, or diarrhea may occur when the dose is excessive.

The Importance of Breathing

It requires a lot of control and concentration not to fall into either panic or ecstasy, in order to feel what the medicine does for the body, brain, and soul. The effect is immediate. It goes to the center of the brain, to the pineal gland, and from there expands molecularly to all the cells of the body. Breathing is of vital importance, as it helps control the sensation of vertigo. It is a process where the sensation of death arrives at a given moment. However, if one accepts it and let's her- or himself go, wholly without fear or thinking, the sensation of death is converted instead into the best of life, of strength and energy and health, that fills your body through vital oxygen. It is something paradoxical and difficult to explain.

Processes After Smoking Otac

Dissolution into fractals, evaporation of sense of self

A sensation of being transported by a white light at the speed of light; the appearance of beings and different manifestations of energy

A feeling of oneness and love for the principles that organize the universe; the intuition that all of life boils down to this very time and space; the need to let go of identity

Complete disintegration of ego and personality and the dissolution of all that is, and the resonance with oneness, God, and absolute consciousness

The restructuring of all the "parts" that constitute the individual; the reinsertion of ego

A repossession of the physical body and the dissipation of the effects of 5-MeO-DMT

A period of intermediary resonance between the two worlds and the complete return to the "normal" state prior to the experience

Remembering Your Encounter with Otac

Is it not important to remember what happens during your experience with the toad medicine. The act of inhaling the vapor and the ceremony that surrounds it is simply the experience we need to have in order to achieve what is beyond experience. Once you've taken the medicine into your body, you will have the ability to re-create, quite vividly, that same set of effects and benefits without necessarily needing an additional trigger or dosage. You must keep in mind, we are partaking of the Otac's gifts not for the alteration of consciousness, but rather to reach higher consciousness through the activation of those sensors.

Sustainability of the Toad Medicine

The only danger for the toads are humans and the way that the humans think.

There are thousands of the Otac toads in the Sonoran Desert, perhaps millions of them. Nevertheless we need to protect their environment. They are unique to this area. Climate changes are affecting the cycle of rain in the desert.

If, instead of trying to control nature, we learn how to live according to the rhythm of nature, then, there will be enough toads and medicine for all the humans on this planet. Remember, to extract their sacred substance, you don't need to trap the toads, kill them, or keep them in captivity. This medicine is perfect the way it is. We just simply need to harvest the medicine every year and then leave the toads alone. Thus, if we don't impact the ecosystem of the toads, the medicine should remain plentiful forever.

Synthetic Drugs Versus Sacred Substances

Modern people cannot distinguish the difference between sacred substances and the drugs synthesized by man, which are heartbreakingly destructive and addictive and invade communities from the most underdeveloped to those of the first world. These destructive drugs are deemed illegal by laws that governments enact for our supposed protection. Yet it is those same governments that allow them to proliferate within a framework of hypocrisy and double standards in a corrupt, vicious, sick, and disoriented society that cares nothing about the suffering of others and leaves souls to rot in an insatiable quest for more pleasure and money.

Unlike other forms of tryptamines, the nectar from the Otac toad is not considered by the institutions of Mexico to be an illegal drug; in fact, it can be freely possessed and consumed in most countries. In the Seri Nation, where I have spent years among its people, the formalities necessary to allow safe consumption of the desert toad have been approved. The Seri community has suffered from terrible poverty as well as high rates of addiction to crystal meth, in part because of its location — close to the US border, in a drug trafficking area. As you will discover in Part Three: Otac in the World, I've lived with the Seris and helped many of them beat their addiction to crystal meth via the toad medicine. Still, I wish to be clear that it's not my intention to promote the synthetic production of this nor any other sacred substance. The first and foremost intention here, and in research and scientific work done in the field, is to recognize and validate officially with the governments of the world the true importance of respecting the laws of Nature, and the creatures that are the biological source of true medicine and knowledge.

Despite all the defamation, there is no scientific argument that can substantiate that psycho-integrators are poisonous or can cause irreversible damage to the people who take them, provided they are taken in the right context. There's also no proof of their constituting a public health risk, certainly compared to licit drugs such as alcohol and tobacco. On the contrary, it has been proven that the substance excreted by the Otac, as well as those collected from sacred plants, are exactly the medicines needed by man at this time.

What I mean is, during our lives as human beings we have many different sensations awakened in an organized manner by external events. Emotions are reactions to events. Memories are then stored in the brain in the form of thoughts. The sensations of the body are inherent to our being, which is basically neutral. In other words, it is the spirit that is eternal and conscious, that which feels. Spirit receives what the mind thinks, and what happens in the body is a consequence. Sacred substances such as the toad medicine are stimuli that trigger a reaction in the body, which is interpreted by the brain and then experienced by us as a cascade of feelings and emotions. We may each express this reaction in different ways, but it leaves its imprint — each encounter becomes a chapter in our life history.

Once ingested, sacred plants and the toad medicine produce similar effects among people of different physical conditions. Experiments with animals have also demonstrated an affinity for entheogenic experiences. Cerebral hormones are present in all of us naturally, though the concentrations vary from person to person. Measurements depend on many circumstances, including the reasons and circumstances of administration. Therefore, it's nearly impossible to use just one word or number to describe the many properties of these chemicals. Consequently, the word "drug" does not apply and only serves to confuse and mislead.

In this modern Internet-enriched world, there is no longer a need to be an expert in the field of biochemistry, botany, or other sciences in order to be properly informed of the characteristics, properties, and similarities of these substances. Today there are no real barriers beyond the personal decision one makes between knowledge and ignorance.

Pharmaceutical Drugs Versus Natural Substances

Pharmaceutical drugs, along with addictive street drugs, are the real poisons. They do not heal. Natural "drugs" are the real medicine. Rohypnol, Lexotan, Effexor, Rivotril, Valium, Risperdal, and other expensive so-called "medicines" only cause more harm. The problem with pharmaceutical drugs is that people think they will recover their health or happiness by swallowing a pill. Some start taking one pill and end up taking twenty. Then instead of just having one illness, they now find their entire systems collapsing in the presence of these chemicals. The culture mistakenly thinks it can buy happiness. We need to reeducate ourselves.

Don't get me wrong — I am not against the technological advances that science has provided to humans. I believe in the fusion of nature with technology. I am chiefly concerned with all the daily habits that make people sick and necessitate hospitalization, with conditions that sometimes are really difficult to treat, illnesses that could have been prevented by changing habits. Reincorporating some of these ancient techniques into our lives will improve the quality of our existence, and reconnect us to nature.

Otac and Life's Purpose

When one reaches the ultimate level of inhaling the Otac
vapors, it is possible for fear to take hold but only for a
moment, as it is followed by a great sense of freedom. We
confront some of our worst nightmares such as the sensation
of death or the fragmentation of ego, reason, mental integ-
rity, and the illusion of personal safety. Everything dissolves
in a fractal of time and space, which is why once the
experience is over, the complete integration of the psyche
is perceptible. This is available to anyone who opens his or
her heart and mind to change, to the magnificence of what
is natural, through the experience of the Otac and certain
power plants.

Calm breathing is the first step when looking to reach the
necessary mental peace and we want to be sensible in all situations of life. This is most important for the alternate states of
consciousness and perception of reality, whether individual,
or collective, through self-consumption of psyco-integrative
medicines with the intention of acquiring divination, or for the
cosmic experience obtained through the energetic exchange of
chemical information decoded by our unconscious minds.

I consider life's purpose to be encountering each other and
accepting each other as essentially fluctuating beings in
constant movement and evolution. It's about understanding

what it means to "find" someone with the least amount of effort. You, as a fundamental piece of the All, find yourself in the right place at just the right moment, so something extraordinary will always happen.

The inner voice that has guided these words and all of my life experiences is clear, loud, and sometimes demanding. Yet, the feeling it leaves me with at all times is one of love, relief, peace, and hope. The energy that flows through the body is divine; nothing has to do with the specific culture that we have learned. We are all blessed and supported by a powerful and invincible feeling of safety and strength. We are all capable of generating and accessing this and other states of abundance. It is wellbeing for our lives. I reiterate that through all of my explorations, the one thing I have always found is another part of my being that I did not know of before. I augment my perspective of this reality and even leave it behind, disconnecting myself from this world and entering a different one, expanding the sense of universality. I recognize myself as being part of the educational process yet at the same time, of being the process itself.

As I acknowledge that every experience is a living thing that perhaps exists for a moment, or perhaps is waiting out there, I wonder: Did this occur in the past? The fact is, time is not what we thought. It is not linear, but omnidirectional, and this opens the door to an understanding of the sacredness of life in every sense of the word. The gods of the past and of the future represent complete cohesion and communion. They are interpreted as the knowing union of all creation beginning with the recognition that we are the optimum expression of life. There is no past, present, or future that does not follow the basic laws of the only thing that truly is: Love. Love has a strength that cannot be denied. We constantly manifest all that is felt, thought, and imagined. because everything is possible in the vast field of spirituality. That may sound abstract, but today I know and understand this as basic truth.

PART TWO:

FULL
DISCLOSURE

The Dream of Creating Connection

Spiritual awakening is a natural phenomenon of our times, due to global necessity. It's time; the change is upon us. There are many of us who think similarly, and we know deep down that the truth is one and global. The sands of the interstellar clock are showing us the way to the unification of all paths — all of which lead to the Truth. That truth is about to become the only path there is. The galactic dawn is inevitable.

Time travelers. Space is our playground in this time of change and the rapid evolution of our species. It is the new dawn of consciousness. We are nearing the truth in this present dimension. I am happy, having found myself and my God in an eternal, intimate bond with nature. A philosophy of love, of knowing, is the alchemy of my evolution: going beyond existence to achieve transcendence. This story will serve to explain the existential crisis that catapulted me into my path of growth and understanding. My mission is to send light across the entire globe, wherever the chemical leviathan might have leaked, the addiction to the unnatural, that which destroys the possibility of feeling how I feel right now.

Am I looking to impress my lifestyle onto others? After having lived the other way before, I can say that my love is stronger now and my perspective more detached. I am more, and I understand so much more than I previously could have dreamed. I act in a manner that contributes to my community, to the development of collective consciousness, to world peace, and to cosmic order. I act from a sturdy foundation. Everything written here is true as far as my memory and conscience can serve. I write this because I feel a need to transmit to the world the message I have received and to bear witness to the Otac world project. We must bring life back to suffering human beings, with full support from all those who have succeeded in touching the deepest fibers of their beings. Little by little, nature will guide us.

Here, with all authority and reason on my side, based on previous knowledge and personal experience, as well as an understanding of history and culture that fuses spirituality with the global future, I will tell the story of how I went from the profane and mundane to the divine and ethereal. I'll share how the longest and darkest night was followed by the brightest morning sun and how I had the most beautiful awakening that my imagination could have ever conceived. My story is about how to create the connection between cosmic and personal levels. This is how I became part of collective cosmic consciousness. I began to leave behind the selfish, individualist part of myself that I had always known, understanding that there are always more and better ways to do things. There is always the possibility of growth, of transforming old attitudes and destructive behaviors, for my own good and for the good of those surrounding me.

While going through the process of growth and maturation, which is never-ending, I saw how we are all connected and how we all have incredible capacities that, for some strange reason, we do not practice. There is a connection with Mother Earth and with other living beings, with all that we see and with that which we cannot touch nor measure by scientific means. We never develop our maximum evolutionary level because we live with our true senses and our deepest essence in a dormant state. I now know why we use only a small fraction of our brains, and I am not surprised that we have been unhappy, frustrated, and bitter. It's because we do not live in real time and because we spend our lives as barbarians. With jobs we hate, partners we do not love, debts, complaints, and frustrated dreams, we're always dreaming about tomorrow or someone else's life. We are largely without feeling or understanding or true living. We are regretful for things we have done and not done. Living in yesterday and tomorrow but never here and now, we fail to enter into existence.

The saddest part is we have done all this in the name of supreme power, progress, the creator, Christ, and science. We think we're being pro-civilization and pro-life. Isn't that funny! What an enormous paradox. In the name of God, of our truth, of what has been taught to us and what we have been made to believe, we have driven ourselves and our species to ever greater suffering. We have contaminated the world with our garbage, and now we approach the end of our path only to meet a dead end, all due to our sick perspective.

The way we perceive ourselves and others is reflected in our daily lives, as is the degree of our understanding of the totality of creation and the role we must play in life.

My Story

My Federal Identification Number is 4432857 and my State Identification Number is 7408/08. I am a surgeon and general practitioner who graduated from the University of Guadalajara, where I attended from 1996 – 2002. I practiced professionally at a care center in Punta Chueca in Kunkak Territory, Seri Nation in Sonora, Mexico.

I am above all dedicated to the treatment of addictions with Otac. I have given over eight thousand sessions over the course of nine years, experimenting with bufotenin and 5-MeO-DMT. I have five years' experience administering entheogens, as an alternative treatment for addictions involving ancient techniques of respiration and reconnection to the elements of the planet. I began by treating the problem of meth addiction among the Seris and soon branched out to treating the community as a whole. The real catalyst for starting the Otac project was when I took this medicine to the Seri community and combined it with their traditional chanting. The Seris are one of the thirteen tribes who currently live in the Sonora Desert. They are an autonomous community who count Shark Island, Mexico's biggest island, among their territory. Seri legend says that a yellow being gave them language and their traditional chants. The medicine, which is yellow, originated in these parts. As I've have discussed, it has to have had some historical, transcendental importance for the indigenous peoples of the past.

I organize detox camps, I am an educator in sacred plants, I offer visionary expeditions of consciousness, and I provide aid to schools and rehab centers. I was born in Guzman City in Jalisco the first of January in 1979. The area was called Zapotlan the Great. The area is mainly cattle and farmland. My mother had a couple of bookstores and worked with publishing houses. Over time she became independent.

I weighed 3,800 grams (8.4 pounds). I was the firstborn of two children. My childhood was a happy one, and vacations with my maternal grandparents were happy as well. Grandma Josefina, a very religious woman, would get up and go to church at five-thirty in the morning. She did this every day. She lived on a farm with pigs, horses, and chickens. There was a lot of room to run around, and the air was clean. Family Christmases with my grandma and uncles from Tuxpan were the happiest times of my life. Like many children of that time, I experienced the impact of a changing society, modernity and constant bombardment by mass media, marketing companies and the corporate world. Little by little, I pushed aside the magic of nature and the simplicity of games for the sophistication of toys. The stories I would make up were fantastic. In my imagination, I took amazing trips into space! All I needed to be happy was to eat and sleep and the promise of "who you will be when you're a man, my son." And I really thought I would succeed in life. I compared myself to other kids and tended to feel that I was more capable. I had a big ego, and this has hurt me in different occasions throughout my life. I received the traditional education of most Mexicans and was raised Catholic. My mother, despite not attending church, has always been a woman of faith with firm beliefs and strong values.

My mother met my father while working as a representative for publishers of printed books, and my father, a mechanical engineer and electrician by trade, gave calculus classes in the engineering program at the University of Guadalajara. He was divorced with two children from his first marriage. My mother had only had one previous boyfriend, so the first real man in her life would be my father. My grandparents, Guillermo and Josefina Hinojosa, did not approve of this liaison since my father had had a past and, a little after my brother David was born, my parents divorced. The last fifteen years of my father's life were dedicated to homeopathy, and quite successfully. Unfortunately, he contracted hepatitis C then developed cirrhosis and died at the age of fifty-two.

Ever since I was a small child, imagination was my tool for diversion, games, and fun. It was very powerful and the perfect toy. It would take me places and show me realms of magic. My mind was always able to keep me busy doing things that I liked, and it was in the simplest things that I would find the most beauty, such as playing with my brother and making cities or game boards with clay, toy cars, and chalk. Since my mom had a bookstore and an office supply store, imagine all the things we had at our fingertips to play with and create worlds with. She was and is a loving, noble, hardworking, honest woman, more so than I can express.

I did not feel the absence of my father when I was a child, but his presence undoubtedly would have been beneficial.

When I transferred schools, the change was enormous.

We were taught to respect others and the values of study and dedication, and commitment and devotion were glorified. I started playing basketball when I was twelve. I was of a decent size, although I did not have the proper body to play. I practiced enough to develop a good technique for dribbling, shooting, and passing the ball. Mental strategy and perseverance began to be noticeable with every move.

My existential crisis and problems came when I became a teenager. It was a time of many internal changes, many emotional conflicts, doubts, and contradictions. I began to define myself, and the actions I took at that age marked me for the rest of my life.

First Time Getting Drunk

A somewhat strange series of events led to the first time I experienced drunkenness. One of my memories takes me back to being nine or ten years old when my cousin Ivan and my brother David began to sneak around and make cocktails when our mothers would leave us alone. It was obvious that at some point, despite our trying to hide the evidence, we were going to be found out. And that's what happened. To top things off, we had been singing a rendition of "La Cucaracha" about a cockroach that had no marijuana to smoke. So our mothers bought us a bottle of rum and a box of cigarettes and dared us to do it in front of them.

We became very dizzy and nauseous, and then began the singing and screaming. Then came the regretting, the throwing up, and the passing out. Next day, the terrible, harsh reality of things settled in: the headache, the dehydration, the stomach trouble, the diarrhea, and the absolute certainty that I never wanted to experience anything like that again. It wasn't until much later when I wanted to look good in front of girls and reaffirm my manliness among my male friends that I would again disfigure my body and consciousness with alcohol.

ADOLESCENCE

This was a very difficult part of my life in which I was confronted with the darkness of dependency to the sensations offered by street drugs. This is the story of how I fell into momentary escape from reality, how dulling it was, and how it hurt me. The unusual euphoria of drugs, the joys of the visions of the altered state in which nothing worries us, where everything is comfort and happiness — that is the experience until the trip changes and everything becomes a nightmare.

The first testimony of healing via Otac is my own. In this story I went from being a perfect child to falling into the trap of drugs, moving from alcohol to illegal drugs and psychoactive substances. That fall was even more painful and difficult as I was a student in a Salesian school where discipline and Catholic education were venerated. Also the high social status made my fall a bit pricklier.

Later I enrolled in high school and began to adopt an attitude that was not the healthiest due to wanting to feel accepted by a new social group. Drinking alcohol and smoking cigarettes were the first steps to please the girls, to feel older and cooler, imitating TV and movies. At first it wasn't too serious, but since parties have everything, and since I had no limits and didn't know much of anything, it was easy for me to go deeper. I was already showing signs of excess. There was a moment where sex and alcohol no longer satisfied me. I wanted something more. That was the feeling then: a constant search, an insatiable hunger to have, to receive, to feel, and of course, to experiment. I so badly wanted to fly and had so many wishes to fulfill, so many desires and frustrations.

Marijuana became the medicine that my crazy brain began to use to feel balanced. The first few times I smoked, I felt a warmth that went through my entire body, my eyes popped, and their corners turned red. I will never forget the first time I smoked cannabis. It was astonishing to feel ideas surging through me. My perception of time was altered and I felt like I was floating. I saw the floor as being very far away. I was elevated. It was magical. My sense of humor was exaggerated. I was constantly laughing. Classic symptoms, of course. I was inebriated without having to drink alcohol.

The feeling was so encouraging, I assumed all drugs were the same and began the path of broad experimentation. It would be years before any substance felt as unique as cannabis, but because it was so easy to experiment, when I was offered inhalants, I accepted. Then came psychotropic pills (benzodiazepine, mainly) and finally, cocaine. Now

I understand that all these street drugs are poisons that imprison, destroy, and enslave lives. They have nothing to do with the magic of sacred medicinal plants, but it would be years before I learned that.

Due to my increased abuse of these substances, I had a very problematic adolescence and my old friends pulled away from me. Soon I was mostly talking to drug users. The social and family stigma that this produced left deep marks. Incorrect information, obsolete beliefs, and taboos became a part of my reality. School for me was effortless and didn't feel like I had to really challenge myself. Being possessive and obsessive is another personality trait that I've had for as long as I can remember. A constant and exhaustive struggle began in my nuclear family. My mother, an excellent woman, always sought for her children education, love, and anything else within her reach. Now she saw before her eyes one of her worst fears: her oldest son was being destroyed by addiction.

Day Zero

The day the bomb was dropped was the day I went to my cousin Ivan's house. He had already had some experiences with cannabis, cocaine, and benzodiazepines he had found in his grandmother's house, prescribed for her son. Ivan found it easy to steal his sick uncle's pills (Clonazepam 2 mg). Then we began to drink beer, smoke marijuana, and inhale cocaine. I took the first pill; two minutes went by and I felt nothing. So I decided to take another two. By the end of the afternoon I had taken seven. I don't know what happened after that; I lost track of everything. I woke up in my bed, couldn't remember a thing, and my poor mother didn't know what had happened to me. I knew then what it meant to completely and entirely black out. I had fried my brain, undoubtedly, so they called my father, whom I rarely saw. Later I learned that his first words were "irreparable brain damage." I can't even imagine what my poor mother must have felt then. As the days went by, the effects began to disappear, but I was never again seen the same by my family, or by myself. I was a "drug addict." In fact, it was years before I felt like my head could work like it had before that experience. (It was through the toad medicine, thanks to the nectar of the toad, that the puzzle pieces finally began to come together once more.) So from being Octavio, an example of intelligence, I was now a product of sadness and shame, of anger and frustration.

Then came my college years. I will never forget my first day of class in the field of surgical medicine and obstetrics in the University Center for Health Sciences. I met a beautiful Asian-looking woman. Her name was Sugeli. She was the first person I spoke to that day in Module O on the second floor. I was struck by her eyes. I had never met a woman like her. We began to talk, became friends, and two months later Sugeli and I were dating. I really enjoyed her company. I spent my time with her laughing. She made me incredibly happy during that time of my life, and before long we were married.

At first, medical school was disappointing in many ways. Of course, due to my countercultural ways, my excessive drinking and my smoking of cigarettes and marijuana, I was completely disrespected as a student and by my peers. In the following semesters, I managed to recover some lost time. I dedicated myself to studying fiercely and obsessively. During the semesters after that, normally the most difficult ones for everyone else, I was ahead of my peers due to my commitment to service, the attention I offered patients and, above all, the humane treatment that has characterized my professional practice ever since.

Another crucial point in my life was the death of my father. I was very sad, of course, and something else happened that was unexpected: I felt the need to become a father myself. My time in medical school passed, and the moment came to do social service work. The grand auditorium of the University of Guadalajara was jam-packed. The students there were already intern doctors and were there to learn our first assignments outside of school. By then, Sugeli and I had a baby and a dog. We were a family and, luckily, the doctor in charge of distributing social services had the consideration to send my wife and me to the same town. So in my first car, a '69 VW Sedan, we drove to the picturesque village of Tuxcacuesco, Jalisco. The arrival of my son had helped me change. He has been my biggest blessing and most beautiful gift. It was a dream year for me. In social service work, I could really feel the value and importance of what I was doing as a doctor in the community. The calm I felt living in the small village gave me the impulse I needed to return to nature and recognize the joy of simplicity and stability.

In Tuxcacuesco I made one great friend: Fernando. I am profoundly grateful to Fernando for his friendship and support. We enjoyed a feeling of constant improvement and training on that campus. Lalo is another good friend, and we too were mates in our volunteer work. The days were long and the shared moments pleasant, and that is how one of the most sincere and beautiful friendships I have had began. Lalo was a friend with a good heart, and we had a lot in common, such as our affinity for sacred plants and nature. Later, in a discussion about peyote, which I was unfamiliar with but which Lalo knew, he described peyote as a master plant that has a spirit and connects you to the remainder of creation. Later, he also told me about psychoactive mushrooms.

Inevitably, I began to read *The Teachings of Don Juan: A Yaqui Way of Knowledge* by Carlos Castaneda. I read without really understanding what the author was saying. I admit that it was not until I read the book a third time ten years later that I understood very much.

In the following months I went to another town with my wife so that we could remain together. When we went to Tonaya, everything changed. I could no longer keep my extra job as a teacher, and the money ran out. To solve our money issues, I began to sell cocaine. I look back on those times with shame. But back then, I believed my coke habit to be normal and even sophisticated. Coke was seen by society as superior to marijuana, and besides, it generated revenue. Today I consider cocaine to be a poison, a total waste of time and a money sponge, an enslaving agent of the mind, body, and spirit — a true illness that must be cured.

My way of repairing the damage I have done, that I was an accomplice to, is through all the work I have done with addicts through Otac medicine. But to get to that point, I had to go through many processes. Once again I bow to the sacred plants and amphibian that forever changed my life.

My First Divine Journey

Some years passed before my path first crossed with *Salvia divinorum*, the first entheogen that I experimented with. The experience was intense; I suppose it was similar to an epiphany. It was a beautiful moment in my life. That is why I eventually named my daughter after it. I remember first meeting Gerry, a young man who emanated light, wisdom, and strength. His energy captivated me instantly and we began an incredible friendship. This friend would be a powerful influence in my destiny, such as no other. One day, Gerry invited me to his house and we sat on the carpet with a third person. He took out his pipe and said, "Hold on to your seat and enjoy the ride." He offered me Maria Pastora (salvia). I indicated that this "wasn't my first rodeo" and asked for a bigger dose. "No, this is enough, I can assure you. Inhale and hold it as long as you can," Gerry told me. He didn't have to say it again because when I started to exhale the first puff, I began to feel like everything was connected through the electric charge within things. Everything had orange metallic borders, and I could see electricity running through the electromagnetic exterior of all that exists. There are no words to describe the beauty we may find in these special states. Those images will remain in my memory forever. They go with me everywhere.

My entire frame of vision broke into fractals that exploded over and over into bright colors: blue, gray, purple, and green. Then some kind of intergalactic highway took me into a luminous whirlwind of incredible velocity and perfect order. I understood that hyperspace is within and we are part of an enormous All, filled with movement from different planes and dimensions. Definitely, other realities alternate in this universe. They emit light that for me translates into feelings, ideas, and images in my mind. I felt in touch with older siblings who'd been waiting for me and that I, somehow, had already been to the expansive spaces I now visited. They transmitted a feeling of wellbeing and safety into me that I had never felt before. I felt intensely happy and included in something important. The experience was part of a whole that was also part of something huge. That sensation of belonging has never left me. Little by little, the ray of light began to disappear and just as quickly as I was sent away, I was sent back to the room with my two friends. My expression of surprise was obvious. I had just had an unforgettable experience, one that marked me for the rest of my life, that introduced me to a magic that continues to touch me and surprise me every day. The first thing that came out of my mouth was, "I want more."

Sacred plants are very interesting.

Peyote

The next experience was peyote. On December 26, 2002, we were going toward Real de Catorce, a remote place in the Mexican desert. The night before I had done cocaine, a habit that I had been dragging along since high school. Back then, I simply could not conceive of a vacation without "blow." This trip I did it with my friends Memo and Gerry, along with Jimbo and La Negra, their two Labradors.

It was New Year's Eve when we went to the Cerro del Quemado and some of the sacred places of the Huichol tribe. We were there, impregnating ourselves with the energy of the land. From the land, some friends got us little balls of mescaline for our return home that same night.

When the time came, we threw the rubberlike material into our mouths. It's a celestial chewing gum of great power, though due to its fibrous texture a bit painful to chew. When this substance touches you, its strength is incomparable. Your body hurts and you feel like you're going to vomit, which you don't know whether to repress or allow. That is the first symptom that the plant is beginning to work. Every sacred organism is different.

One of my friends was the first to declare he was seeing visuals, while I, on the other hand, felt and saw nothing. Suddenly there was a strong pang of pain and an intense need to evacuate. The strength with which I expelled the matter, and accompanying sounds and gases, made my entire being vibrate. It was the most intense intestinal liberation I have ever experienced. I saw what came out, something that was moving and seemed somehow alive, slimy, and evil. I felt the need to do it again and again. When that first reaction passed, followed by uncontrollable laughter, I realized that my surroundings had changed. I saw a speckled starry night around us. The howling of coyotes reminded me of my own fragility in the dark winter night in the middle of the desert. I was completely high. I was feeling the effects of the mescaline. I remember wanting to build a fire, but it was impossible as we couldn't tell the dry branches from the live ones. They all looked blue, and it was disconcerting.

After the ritual of ingesting the cactus and containing the nausea through complete concentration, I tried to channel my thoughts into a medical explanation for the foaming reaction that peyote had when in contact with stomach acid. Due to the challenges that peyote represents, it is considered by many to be a plant of initiation into shamanism for the understanding of consciousness, through which a mental state can be reached of dopaminergic stimulation. Wise men say that the use of peyote is a sacred ritual and once one accesses this medicine, there is personal growth and a cleansing of the heart. It then becomes a sweet, friendly plant that will take you by the hand to the most fantastic and amazing landscapes you can imagine. Then suddenly I couldn't handle it anymore. It was too much peyote for me. I began to vomit, and I was no longer in that dry place under the scorching sun when I lifted my face. I had been transported to the bottom of the ocean, with enormous animals that I had never seen before. I was underwater, yet I could see everything. How was this possible?

The sound of a motorcycle engine brought me back to reality. I turned around to see that my friend and I were connected, seeing the same thing. Kaleidoscopic images with colors that changed in front of our eyes, with beautiful geometric shapes and such grace and forms as are inconceivable by the human imagination. (An important fact to share here is that all the white fuzz must be taken off the cactus, as it contains strychnine, a muscular paralyzer. This is not a reaction you need to be feeling in the middle of the night in the desert.)

Finally, we started back with our friends and were barely aware of the long uphill journey and the many miles traveled. Time had flown since eleven o'clock the previous night. It was now five in the afternoon of the next day. We had not eaten or drunk water. When I returned, I remember being able to see the auras, intentions, and true personalities of people. I could see their thoughts and feel their emotions. At nighttime, we felt like giants that could touch the stars, looking down on everybody and being able to see in every direction. The lucidity and clarity were especially exceptional. The following days we took hikuli (peyote), nothing but hikuli. In fact, we ended that day in a way I'll never forget. Once again, darkness arrived and we were far from camp without a lamp. Holy mescaline sharpened my reflexes and augmented my strength, the velocity of my movements, the elasticity of my body, and the capacity to make good decisions in a fraction of a second. I felt increased physical capacity like never before. The difference I felt after leaving that place and returning home was shocking.

I still feel that there is great incongruence that I am Mexican and yet it took me twenty-three years to know the sacred plants and regions of my country, while thousands of foreign tourists come to Mexico solely for the purpose of experiencing them.

Two weeks after having returned from the desert, Gerry invited me to Maruata, a beach in Michoacan where an indigenous community lives that speaks Nahuatl. I accepted and thought about taking the rest of the mezca that we'd brought from the desert. We left Guadalajara behind and went south to the state of Jalisco. We were received by some friends who already had a camp set up. There was no one there who didn't have a connection with a very broad agenda of experience, and we ourselves weren't exactly sober, as we had already taken out the little balls of mescaline that we'd brought from the desert near San Luis Potosi. That's when I remembered salvia, which I asked to smoke, and that's when a guy said to me, "Wait here, Guero, I've got just the thing."

He left and returned shortly with a little bulge in his hand that looked like salvia. My friend was the first to try it. His face suddenly changed, and I saw him holding on for dear life to the banana trees, with a wild look in his eyes. Those witnessing laughed at the poor individual. I, assuming I'd experience the same effect as I did when I was with Gerry, made a cigarette with the leftover salvia and began to smoke. I puffed on it three times and began to feel the psychedelic effects. I continued to pull and inhale with all my strength when suddenly colors, electricity, magic, and beauty began to get more and more intense. I did it with the intention of having a good time and getting really "messed up," as young people commonly say. I assumed it would once again be celestial music, colors, and magical feelings. But what actually happened was the most shocking experience of my life.

Within my atheism and arrogance, I found the greatest learning that anyone can have in this world: a truly mystical experience and an actual encounter with the creator. It was a reunion with my true spiritual nature and my true self, with the infinite knowledge of cosmic intention and what we typically call God. The feeling of emptiness and solitude were total and I had never felt so afraid. It was like being in front of the mirror and seeing my beliefs and values shattered. I began to hear a voice screaming in and out of my head. It was the loudest, most clear voice I had ever heard, before or since. I shuddered and began to tremble and cry. He, God, wanted me to hear him and I, without knowing or wanting to, went into places unknown to me where I did not know what to expect. This is what I heard: "I am the Alpha and Omega, the beginning and end, life and death, everything and nothing, I am you, I am he, I am they, I am everyone, I am no one."

In that moment, taken by the hand of that superhuman energy, I was catapulted at the speed of thought by the strongest and most uncontrollable entheogen there is, vertically toward the center of the universe. This nonhuman manifestation let me know that, if I wanted to, I had the opportunity to change my destiny and that of humanity. If I accepted, the reward would be eternal. If I did not, I would go back to my normal life like any other human being. Obviously, this would not come without a price. The ticket to the entrance of that fantastic and marvelous world would be to confront my greatest fears and would have to vanquish evil, that demon that we all have inside ourselves. But once I surrendered, my life would serve as testimony and example of divine strength and love.

When I came back to my body, my throat was hurting and my heart was beating hard at full gallop. The impact of that moment has marked me for life. My immediate reaction was to retreat to a monastery to ask for forgiveness. Every time I remember it, I get goosebumps. Never before or since have I had such a reproach from divine forces.

After traveling that entire night through old Maruata, I was really quite worried since I didn't know, nor do I know to this day, how to explain what had happened. My thoughts went along the lines of, "I'm not the right one for this mission," all the way to, "Don't worry, Tavo, it's just a product of your imagination, nothing more. It's just a game. God doesn't exist." The colors, sensations, thoughts, forms, and shapes that appeared before my eyes that night were endless. The next day, when we woke up, we went to visit the individual who had given me the salvia. When he saw me come back, he seemed amazed, but when he saw me so decided and enthusiastic, he sold me another dose to take to Guadalajara.

But my life after that trip to the beach was never again the same. To begin with, when I arrived in Guadalajara I spoke with my wife with whom I've always had a beautiful relationship. I have nothing but the very best things to say about her. Sugeli is a healthy, educated, responsible, intelligent, and excellent woman who gave me my son. They, my immediate family, were the only thing I loved, my reason for living, and what gave me the strength and desire to go on. I remember saying to Sugeli, "Su! God has spoken to me!"

She thought that I was still high, or that I had gone completely mad. Her amazement was due to her having seen me for years as an atheist who spent his life denying the existence of a supreme being. I believed that life was a product of chance, that there had been a time and place in space where the necessary factors had come together for there to be life. And therein lay its value: its short duration and fragility. That is why I wanted to inhale the world in one breath, why I lived in such a rush. Because I believed you only live once.

St. Sebastian

And there, the three inseparable friends were together,
Gerry, Lalo, and myself. I remember Gerry, the master,
always innovative in taste and style, such as the music he
would share with me back then, which was such an important contribution to my life. He also bore an atmosphere of
magic and emotion that laced our life in those unforgettable
days. When we got to Puerto Vallarta, it was impossible to
walk with so many people. It was Spring Break, with young
people crowding the bars, night clubs, and beaches. People
were everywhere. Looking to escape the crowds, we decided
to go to Sayulita, which was more of an underground hippie
beach good for surfing. Our days were filled with LSD,
ecstasy, marijuana, partying, the beach, and a lot of fun.

On Sunday I turned the car on to pick up Lalo and heard
a strange sound. I went to the mechanic and he said,
"Look, Guero, one of the pulleys is busted. Go buy another
at Bucerias and come back so we can install it." To my
surprise, one of his assistants came with me. When we got
to the shop, I saw two girls with braids who caught my
attention. They were in the middle of the road hitchhiking.
They were from Hermosillo, Sonora, and had come to
Sayulita for the raves.

Those days and nights were fantastic, some of the best of my life, shared with Cecilia, Abril, Enrique, acid, ecstasy, and marijuana on the beautiful beach of Sayulita. It was three weeks of vacation partying. That week I fell in love with Cecilia Encinas Martinez, and I still remember clearly that night of passion before I went back to Hermosillo, Sonora.

Unfortunately, that was the end of my marriage. Also unfortunately, the following weeks when I was without Cecilia, coke took over my life. One day, I was looking for some blow and someone offered me a rock of crack, and I accepted. I remember sweating and shaking after taking that first hit sitting in the bathroom. I thought about how heavy the experience was. An invasion of my ego overtook my body. I knew it wasn't healthy. I had lockjaw and felt myself being poisoned. It was the beginning of the downward spiral that would threaten complete annihilation.

So then the world of hard drugs began. When I arrived with the cocaine in my hand, my friend and partner said he did not want to sell it as powder to be inhaled but as rock to be smoked. So then nothing sold, and our business failed. With no money and all of the goods there, I am sad to confess that my partner and I spent three days and nights smoking crack. By then, the possessive energy of cocaine had me in its claws, in a state of blindness and without coordination of thought. I was at the mercy of my own gorging, which was endless. My body trembled and shuddered with involuntary spasms of the fingers, hands, and feet. My heart had never dealt with so much pressure. I would describe it as someone pointing a gun at my head and threatening to shoot. The fear was horrible. Your worst fears become reality and you become the protagonist of an endless cycle of unfounded panic. Without eating or sleeping, just drinking water and staying high on crack. Panicked. Completely screwed up. No matter how much you smoke, the desire never abates.

It is of vital importance to transmit the information of how dangerous this substance is. Millions of people suffer from this evil. Most of them deny it, especially if they're occasional users. Unlike inhaled coke, the effect of crack is devastating. Blood pressure and heart rate soar, and there is an increase in the plasma concentration of all substances related to stress response and danger.

My First Experience with Magic Mushrooms

Once more, this adventure includes my friend Gerry, who shared his "'shrooms" with me in a village near the southern mountains of Jalisco. He thought it was time that I got to know psychoactive mushrooms, and since this advice came from him, I didn't think twice but only asked how I'd recognize them. He said, "They're only golden-yellow mushrooms that have a purple skirt under the cone on the upper one-third of the stem. They grow on cow dung, so there's no mistaking them."

With this information and with every intention of having the experience, Gerry, Cecilia, and I went to the mountains and stopped at the first picturesque little ranch that we saw. It was straight out of a book illustration with its little cows, green grass, and white clouds against the beautiful, breezy blue sky. I jumped the fence, walked to the ruminants and, after being unsuccessful for a while, saw one and ate it. Ceci found an enormous mushroom so bright gold it shined. Surrounding it was an entire colony of smaller magic mushrooms. Without thinking, I began to eat, filling my belly and filling my shirt, which I was using for a sack to carry the extras in. I was thinking, "Why has no one told me it's this easy?"

In the car, Cecilia ate some and we were soon on our way back to civilization. I began to feel a bit of gas, digestive discomfort, and nausea. I figured my body didn't know how to digest 'shrooms, as I had never eaten them before; besides they were raw and I'd eaten a lot. Suddenly I remembered my first peyote high and expected the worst. Luckily, the effects were not the same. Still, I was so concerned with the stomachache that I stopped the car to evacuate. Then the fear of having poisoned myself with toxic mushrooms invaded me.

I turned to look at the grass and Ceci's face. I lowered my eyes to her left thigh, where she had a pinkish beauty mark about six inches long. It looked like it had just sprung to life. I saw it move away from its original place. I began to feel invaded by a strange feeling — really strange. Suddenly, I felt I was driving over rocks or bumps so I thought maybe we had gotten a flat tire. I began to feel intensely the truck's vibrations and the different engine sounds as though they were an extension of my body. The temperature and oil gauges and the speedometer had all gone crazy. All the lights were blinking on and off simultaneously. The wheel was melting in my hands and everything was liquid. Far away, I could see illuminated beings that were intelligent and obviously not from Earth. They watched me from the distance, as if taking care of me, watching over what I did.

I got really scared. I asked Cecilia, "What's going on? Is something trembling? What's going on with the world? Is everything like this? Does everyone know that things are like this?" I stopped at the edge of the road again, frightened. The beings were gone but I was afraid the police would come along and see me in such a state. They'd surely arrest me, as there was no way to hide that I was tripping.

Once again in the car, I was now watching the landscape go by and crying out of joy. Now past the initial fear, I felt very good. Immensely happy, I thought about Earth, about the countryside and the cows. I loved life and all that existed in the world. I understood the greatness of spirit and the universe. Everything within me took shape and fit perfectly. There was nothing hurtful. Everything felt good, much better than I'd ever realized. Nothing compared to the healing of mushrooms, I decided. The joy would not dissipate. In my room that night I thought already about the next 'shroom trip.

In a sense, I grew up in those green fields that day. Many times as a child I had seen those same mushrooms. Despite my adolescence having been plagued by episodes of intoxication, it was nothing compared to what those marvelous life forms had made me feel. It would have been healthier, definitely, to begin with sacred plants rather than alcohol, psychotropics, marijuana, cocaine, and inhalants.

We owe much to these divine beings, these natural substances, products of cosmic knowledge that have been here on this planet throughout time. Certainly my life, my health, my future, my reality, and those of my loved ones, and all the people who are touched by this healing energy, have been transformed in a very positive way.

The little money I had to my name after separating from my wife was less than 3,500 pesos (about $225, today). Even so, I took off on a trip with Ceci to San Jose del Pacifico in the Sierra Madre Sur in the Mexican state of Oaxaca. Going past Puerto Escondido, we got to Mazunte then Zipolite. We went to see the sunset at Punta Cometa then hiked up to Pochutla, where we took a shortcut through Miahuatlan. With almost no gas, we made all those twists and turns, going uphill.

Finally, after driving nonstop for twenty-eight hours, we arrived at the picturesque little town of San Jose del Pacifico, a beautiful village filled with wooden cabins that smelled of pine trees. There was delicious traditional food and, of course, sacred mushrooms, what the pre-Columbian natives called teonanácatl, flesh of god. There was also a common edible fungus called nanacates, or flesh of the woods. The *teo* prefix in teonanácatl refers to the divine energy that gives us life and that doubtlessly manifests itself when ingesting these mushrooms in adequate form and quantity.

Awaiting Cecilia and me were Gerry and a guy called
El Pelicano. They would present us with a new way of
ingesting mushrooms (*Psilocybe caerulesens*, in this case,
rather than *mazatecorum*): 'shroom tea. We talked while I
drank the tea and the master ate. When I began to feel the
effects, I retired to the bedroom with my girlfriend. I was
exhausted from the journey and the recent change in my
lifestyle, plus the unknown and the known, as well. It was
an experience that I needed to go through in privacy.

I was reminded of the most important thing always:
the planet is alive, it feels, and it communicates with us
through energy and decoded information that the chemical
molecules carry.

We returned to San Jose. My next mushroom session was
very healing and emotionally cleansing. I cried a lot and
phoned Sugeli and asked for her forgiveness from the
bottom of my heart, for everything I had done. She said
that if I wanted another chance I had to leave Cecilia and
come home. I couldn't. It was too important for me to
continue the path I had begun. Sugeli didn't understand
and called me such things as pathological liar, kleptomaniac,
egocentric, manipulative, abusive, opportunist, advantage-
taker, deceitful, treacherous, not really a man, unfaithful,
and tyrant. Before, love, promises, and sweetness. Now it
was the complete opposite. Actions and reactions. Love and

non-love. We pay for everything in this life. My own life
has proven it time and again.

I looked for a job and, at the first interview, was hired as
lead doctor in a pharmacy in Tlaquepaque. Danger: comfort
zone nearby. Within the professional context once again, my
negative, self-destructive side began to reassert itself. Months
earlier I had begun consuming crack again, but now crack
was consuming me. I quickly used up everything in the
pharmacy. Now I had problems with Ceci. I was smoking
crack every day, so she was having to deal with the consequences of my actions. One day, Ceci decided she couldn't
deal with the stress anymore and left for Hermosillo. Living
with a crack addict must be something awful. The stereotyp-
ical tics, the restlessness, psychosis, paranoia — it's enough
to drive anyone insane.

In those difficult months, I returned to the desert of
Wirikuta, where I hoped to find a cure for my addiction.
The trip began in the early morning in a thick fog. It was
like time-travel. The desert is a magical and incredible place,
seasoned with many helpful substances, but I did not find
a lasting cure. While I was away from the city, I stopped
thinking about crack, but when I went back I quickly
used up the pharmacy. In my desperation to obtain more,
I became a mule, or transporter, risking my car and my

freedom for a few rocks. I soon crashed my car and again was looking for a job.

I went to a few interviews, one of them at a private rehab and eating disorders clinic. To my surprise, they gave me the job as medical director. As another surprise, I found the wife of a friend as a patient there. Life puts us in strange and funny situations. The woman and I once partied together, and now I was an addicted medic and she was an addicted patient.

One thing I did not like about these types of businesses, rehab clinics, is that the therapies are meant to prolong the patient's stay and perpetuate their suffering, enslaving them to a further need to medicate. Since I did not want to continue to be an accomplice of that system, I left the place.

I went to Maruata. It was a trip to forget. Gerry cooked some rocks and we smoked them. I was bitter, desperate, and feeling like I was in a ditch. I had lost everything: my pride, my health, my job, my wife and son, and now my girlfriend. I accused myself: "All this craziness just to follow some voice! I was crazy! What the hell happened to me? At what moment did lunacy overtake my life? How did my reality become one of vice and failed friendships? How do I possibly recover? Where is the light now, the magic of the natural world?"

Crack gave me years of walking aimlessly around the streets of Guadalajara, without a dime in my pockets, without eating or sleeping for days, without bathing for weeks, caught in an endless cycle like so many people in the world.

During this aimless existence, I visited my mom and begged for her forgiveness. I finally landed a job. I lived humbly to save money. Since it was a decent paycheck and a comfortable schedule, I looked for an apartment to no longer be in my mother's house. The mistake was living three blocks away from where they sold crack. I was in that neighborhood for a few months. During that time, I had the opportunity to find out about various private rehab centers. I saw the gravity of the situation that is the use of drugs in our society. Most patients end up being medicated for long periods of time, without getting back their health or freedom, without self-sufficiency or independence. I sadly proved to myself the inefficiency of treatment clinics. They keep people sick with their illnesses, controlling them but never curing them. I noticed that it took a minimum of three months to detox the body, but there is a huge tendency to relapse and continue drug use.

Those working in the pharmacy proposed a project called Freedom and Family Integration, a rehab clinic that would approach the problem differently. The plan was to evolve the typical residence houses, highlighting the importance of a healthy diet, exercise, occupational therapy, and, most importantly, avoiding the use of prescription drugs in treatment. For this project I went to live in Jocotepec. The houses rented by the investors were large and expensive. The place had once been a hotel with three separate buildings.

I was happy for a year, and Ceci returned to me. But I was so absorbed by work that I neglected Ceci and suddenly, she got pregnant. I completely objected at first, but then I thought about it and agreed to support her because of the love I felt — though I knew that it would mean the end of our relationship. Between the demands of my job and my relationship, there was a moment when I felt like I would go crazy, but I felt a sense of responsibility, so I put my personal problems aside. Unfortunately, only a few months later, the group of investors dissolved, and soon we didn't have enough money for the payroll. We began downsizing. Employees were leaving, and then it got to the point where I was all alone with my commitment to the clinic and all the work that it entailed.

This chapter of my life ended with an image very popular in Mexico in 2006: the first game of the Mexican soccer team in the World Cup. That turned out to be the right moment for an important friend to re-enter my scene. As always before, his charm and humor made him an incredible teacher for me, teaching me to sit face-to-face with the enemy, look him in the eye, and see him for what he is, to smoke from the same pipe, but not the one of peace and tranquility, but to taste his more powerful and addictive essence and to understand it as flawed love, a terrible, jealous girlfriend. That is the nature of cocaine powder, and especially crack.

Arrival of the Toad

This friend I refer to — Gerry — arrived one day saying he had "brought the medicine." He took out a glass bulb and put it in front of my face, and the first thing I thought was, "Oh no. More garbage. I'm already fucked up enough. I don't want to know about anything else."

But my friend insisted, and he sounded pretty convincing. "Just take a hit. Don't be scared. This is going to make you better." He lit up, the bulb made cracking noises, and smoke came out. Now count to twenty. "One, two, three, four… "

I don't remember getting to fifteen. I began to see electrical currents running across my entire frame of vision and throughout my body. I was surprised to feel so many emotions. In general, I was both pleased and afraid. I thought the substance was similar to a strong LSD trip at the height of the experience, or to enhanced *Salvia divinorum*, or maybe to mushrooms at the climax of the 'shroom experience. I had a lot of questions, but also a lot of fear because the experience was so intense. I really thought it was going to be the last time and that I "died" while high on a substance.

In my head, meanwhile, I began to feel a clarity that amazed me. Everything vanished into thin air, but what remained constant was my consciousness. I felt healing energy entering my body. At the same time, all the toxins were exiting my body through the pores. I felt that I had a second shot at life. This time, I decided, I was going to take advantage of it. Excuse the cliché, but I saw the light at the end of the tunnel. I felt my heart beat strongly again, my eyes were clear and bright with light, and my poor lungs filled with oxygen once again. It was a state of peace and relaxation unlike any other I had ever experienced. In fifteen minutes, I was reborn. As incredible as that may seem, it was true.

What I had smoked was toad medicine.

Thanks to you, little Sonoran toad, and to Gerry, and most importantly, to God, those fifteen minutes saved my life, and there's no price that can be put on that.

However, I needed a lot of the nectar to heal, and at first I didn't really know what that material was. But, thanks to the nectar, I have succeeded in rebuilding a meaningful life. To this date, it's been seven years since I last smoked crack, since I was a complete, hopeless crackhead.

This sense of relief and strong feeling of gratitude toward the universe has stayed with me. It was a long journey to get here, one filled with suffering, pain, and craziness, but in the end, with the poetic justice of life, sprinkled with the sense of humor of my creator, it's all been worth it. The

strength of the cosmic, universal, and eternal light over-
comes evil and darkness, as the work of the magic of nature
and creation.

Since then, I have not hurt my body again. I respect life
and the creative manifestation that is the beautiful energy
provided to us all, that is found everywhere forever within
us. In each of us are the answers to all the questions and the
potential to reach the rebirth of the healing holotherapeutic
psycho-integratives through entheogens that open the doors
to the wonders and the unknowns of life. Through the
field of visions and mental projections I realized that this
experience was what I had needed. I knew this was the gift
promised by the voice I heard in Maruata.

In the years that followed, I've become more involved with
the sacred toad nectar. After a year of struggle and sacrifice,
I was presented with the opportunity to go to Oaxaca and
pursue the dream, thanks to the financial help of Mrs. Vann
and an '86 Range Rover, a powerful 4x4 automobile. Along
with a crew of others, I headed to San Jose del Pacifico.
Before leaving, I met Evan and Corbis, friends who had
shown Gerry how to get the toad substance in a cultural
exchange. A helpful doctor took us to the mycelium of
fungus, and they showed him a video of the procedure.
They sold grams and sessions, but they wouldn't tell anyone,
including me, what the substance was. All I knew was that

the active ingredient was DMT. So with only that information, and with the books of Terence McKenna at hand, we
all guessed that we were smoking ayahuasca. But we were
mistaken. Finally we had to go to Sonora to investigate.

On the twenty-fifth of July, 2006, my daughter Salvia Rettig
Encinas was born, and that day we went to the desert to
pick up the secret ingredient of our magic formula. We went
to Sonora that same afternoon. We only had 2,500 pesos,
a kilo of mushrooms, and some LSD. We got to Guamuchil,
and that's as far as our budget got us. We made some calls
and managed to get a loan of five hundred pesos, which got
us as far as San Carlos.

We looked for magic toads in various places and collected
the substance during the following three nights. There
were hundreds of toads eating insects under the moonlight.
Despite having in my bag the possible solution to my addictions, I also had some reservations. Over the years, I had
developed caution, mistrust, and a bit of incredulity. Still,
we accomplished our mission under the starry night of the
Sonoran Desert then continued on our journey to Nogales
with the medicine in our hands.

In Nogales we picked up my daughter and my beloved
ex-wife, then returned finally to Guadalajara with no further
incidents. It's important to note, in regard to entheogens,

that the more you consume, the less effect it has since, just
like cannabis, it loses its magic and purpose with use. For
me, it meant being free of cocaine and was a breath of
life for my brain and spirit. I wanted to share the experience with others in the same circumstance. Because of
that, I began to frequent rave parties with the intention of
spreading information about the toad. I wanted to end all
the misconceptions about smoked ayahuasca or vegetable-
sourced DMT. I spoke with honesty at every turn, with no
more interest than simply spreading the message of light
and hope, helped by this powerful molecule of God. In the
process of my own healing, the message of the plants was to
bring to as many people as possible the information found
in natural organic chemical components, and good quality
cannabis was doubtless a tool that helped. Five months
went by in which I slowly recuperated from cocaine addiction. I was eager to start using the new medicine. I didn't
know what I needed to do, but I knew I was supposed to
do something.

COMBINING ENTHEOGENS

For some time I tried healing my soul, body, and spirit from self-induced intoxication and poisoning. On various occasions, I combined the Otac nectar with *Salvia divinorum* to heal myself from the substance that had nearly destroyed me. I also used lysergic acid (LSD). Sometimes the experiences were terrifying, as though I had lost all reason. At other times I felt complete calm with 5-MeO-DMT. The horrible panic of crack would sometimes shoot through, and when I was at the most critical point, I would add more *divinorum*. I felt everything very strongly. Many times I ended up crying and asking for forgiveness. Little by little, these sessions allowed me to completely detach myself from wanting to use cocaine, until I finally reached the point of completely abandoning it.

The process of my rehabilitation, and the healing that took place after, lasted eighteen months. It took me many sessions of working with the medicine to overcome my addiction. The sheer amount of synthetic substances I had placed in my body over the years had left me deeply intoxicated and I needed lots of medicine to quit completely.

The difference was in keeping myself busy working twelve-hour days, which was important for generating income. From the moment I arrived in Hermosillo, the city where I had grown up, a place of exceptional weather and beauty. I was working. My job was with an important chain of clinics that provided low-cost health care. It was this work that established the practical foundation for what I do today. I was doing everything as competently as I could, always giving my best, working honestly and honorably. That is how my mind began to calm. The anxiety and desperation to use cocaine began to diminish for seconds at a time, until the seconds became minutes, then hours, then days, then weeks and months, and finally years.

Once I was free of the crack addiction, I started performing informal research with people addicted to different drugs to see if my success with Otac resulted from my openness to change or if there was something about the toad medicine that had real healing properties. I had completely overcome facets of my personality that had tormented me for so long. Now I wanted to serve as a bridge to bring this same state of balance into the lives of others.

With the passing of the months, the rain showers arrived. I gathered a lot of medicine, but sessions were sporadic. Yet the number of interested people constantly increased. It was during that time that I met Lupillo, a user of crystal meth, cocaine, marijuana, various pills, and other crazy intoxicants, but with one toad session he dropped it all. It has now been over two years since he last used street drugs.

I also remember Luis Angel, who'd been in prison for a few years. There's a lot of meth and cocaine in prison. When Luis Angel got out he continued to use these drugs regularly. He never had enough money for his habits, though, and his problems at home were constant. Finally, after one session with *Bufo alvarius*, Luis Angel found the solution. His life came into proper focus and his business prospered. He suffered health problems but found the peace and balance needed to heal his life. I could recite the case of another close friend who had HIV yet found the strength, through his experiences with Otac, to go back to school and graduate at the top of his class in graphic design.

Those who were before seen as vagabonds or social parasites are working and finding ways to move ahead, personally and globally, in total peace and harmony with the universe, thanks to sacred medicines such as that of the toad.

I was further inspired to investigate this possibility when one day, when I was working as a physician, I discovered a spider bite on my leg. It became quite painful, so I took the toad medicine to get a good night's sleep. I woke up the next morning and my leg was 80% better. This revelation, coupled with my curiosity triggered by my recovery from my addiction, prompted me to go to the authorities to seek approval for using the toad medicine on others. The authorities encouraged my research and asked me to continue and collect testimonials. Then, I was invited by the Seri community to try it on them.

I have enjoyed every second of my new life in these lands. I found a very honorable job with the B.E.S.T Foundation. With its help, I have been able to aid many people. I have a long history of consultations and have received the distinction of the Gold Robe of Worth and Service. I've made a lot of friends and have helped all of them. I feel happy and fulfilled. Everything in my life is harmonious. I am light and I am love. I am a spiritual and eternal being. I am God and I say it with all humility, with the certainty that I am not just an ordinary being. Just like a rock, or any other form of life, we are each a god, for there is divinity in everything. For every mistake made, I want to offer actions of benefit for my community. Mistakes made in the past, in the present or in the future, are products of my ignorance, of my immaturity, of my stupidity. They are never the product of cruelty or of active awareness.

I'm not trying to speak of my adventures in a boastful way. I remember and share what I have done, what I have seen, felt, and lived because it was my objective to experience honestly and be able to say at the end of my days with certainty, "I know because I lived it."

Dissatisfaction and the Desire for More

The point of no return is now close at hand: an extinction that seems to have already begun. Global warming, deforestation, and a high demand for energy that draws from reserves of combustible fossils now running out — there's a long way to go with regard to clean sources of energy and worldwide structural changes based on planetary wellbeing. There is only one energy source and one living being. If we do not learn this quickly, history (if anyone lives to write it) will name us responsible for complete destruction of all that the cosmos gave us.

You may be asking yourself, "How is all of this related? What does one thing have to do with another?" Well, it's simple. For me, the future is promising and full of possibilities; I have visualized it as such. That is how I feel and that is how I live. What I expect from the world comes from my own feelings of fulfillment and wellbeing. I do not aspire to the "should be," nor do I seek to possess. I only Am, and by that token I enjoy it all.

In my past I had read about and met people who said they were at peace, while others truly showed it. Personally I did not know unrest and therefore could not value peace. My perspective deepened with time, with experience, including experimentation with sacred plants and various medicinal substances. I experienced extreme stimulation to my central nervous system with methamphetamine and cocaine, which can produce panic and fear comparable to the feeling of imminent death. I also sampled many states of consciousness induced by various neurotransmitting molecules. Landslide mushrooms, LSD, and Otac all offer unique states of consciousness. The visions I experienced were spectacular, reminding me of the Greek and Aztec figures that I had seen in books and photographs of archeological zones. Colors were experienced in high definition and sharpness.

I was increasingly able to see clear differences between what I had read in medical and scientific texts and what I learned through years of experiences with a variety of doses and applications of ancient medicines. The result was a general domino effect leading to a state of joy, of complete peace and harmony with the cosmos and the fundamental process of creation.

From the moment I began my studies in the organic sacraments until today, the general panorama seems to have improved significantly. I took a glimpse behind the surfaces and saw a haze of widespread complacency and control of the masses, and I understand with certainty, or believed I did, how a quiet, personal sense of fullness and centeredness comes. Now I flow with the controlled movement of life energy itself. Evolution is a time warp if we connect with the primary portal. This is the maximum sensation that a living organism can bestow upon another, uniting him or her with the origin of existence itself (despite its being a fantasy created by our consciousness). Now we understand that everything has an answer in the end. There are poisons and antidotes, just as there are illnesses and ways to heal them. We are born healthy; it is the system of the modern world that makes us sick. It is society that is ill, and it is society that is the illness. Only you can heal yourself and it will be all of us together who end said disease with humility and caution, with reason on our side and all of creation behind us — and with one clear objective: wellbeing.

The only thing necessary to be happy and healthy is consistent balance imbued with the soaring frequencies of spirituality and the company of all the natural elements.

The Moral of the Journey

No one can live for others. We each have our own path and destiny. At the end of the day, we will all go to the same place. The only thing we will leave behind is our legacy, and all we will take will be our memories, emotions, and experiences.

It is a human failing that we have strayed so far from our origin, especially those of us who can see that we will return to the place we all came from, expanding consciousness, oneness with reality. If it hadn't been for the toad, I surely would have died years ago from my addiction. The toad medicine helped me regain consciousness in good health, and it was common sense that propelled me to move on, to leave behind all that hurt or offended my spirit.

The years that have followed my life of complete rehabilitation have been very different. I've gained a lot of confidence and security. Stability and peace allow for hard work on a constant daily basis, and that has been great. I found the love of creation. I've also experienced the infinite love of God. I have received him, and that can only be good news for my loved ones. We are all light and darkness. In our interior we have learned about the absence of God. Yet even in the darkness of the longest and coldest night, the infinite love of the divine essence remains.

PART THREE:

OTAC
IN THE
WORLD

The Otac Experience:
Fusing Reality and Fantasy

In his book *DMT: The Spirit Molecule*, psychiatrist Dr. Rick Strassman wrote about the first study of hallucinogens in the United States more than twenty years ago, in which he administered forty intravenous doses to sixty volunteers over a time period of five years. Many of these volunteers reported experiencing similar effects. Strassman's work confirmed that there is no longer any reason to prohibit the study of these substances as there is no data indicating toxicity in the subjects studied, no indication of undesirable or permanent side effects. In every case, the duration of the effects was similar and the individuals reacted in similar ways to the dosage. I believe it is important to conduct similar studies with the Otac nectar, which, despite belonging to the same group of substances called tryptamines, is differentiated by a molecule more commonly found in preparations with DMT (it is the N in N-DMT).

Despite its different effects, I find greater therapeutic value in the secretion of the Sonora toad than in any other entheogen compound, due to its short duration and its incredible potential. These qualities make it my number one candidate for biopsychosocial medicine, as a change promoter, and for improving the quality of life.

Otac is the transducer between reality and fantasy, and creates a hybrid state in which both may manifest together. It is a direct path to the most extraordinary and unbelievable states that could ever be produced in the human being. In my particular case, it was truly incredible to breathe in the vapor produced by the nectar of the Otac. It opened the door for me to understand who I am, who we all are, where I come from, and where we are going. It gave me the opportunity to consciously choose my destiny, to value what this game called life is about. And, as unbelievable as it may seem, this is reality. I have lived it and shared it with many people. Close to eight thousand sessions have been given in various countries of the world. I've found that people in all parts of the world think the same way. It is not just me. It is the toad. It is the substance. It is the expanded state gifted to anyone who wants to open his or her heart and mind to the change that can happen through this divine energy. It is a well-deserved gift. I have dedicated nine years of my life to studying, diffusing, and experimenting with the properties of *Bufo alvarius*. My only aim is to do what is right. I know how good it feels to do what one can, what one must, what one thinks is best on the broadest level.

Otac is a teacher medicine. It allows you to have a dialogue with yourself, helping you to see yourself from many different angles, which reveals so much intelligence and knowledge inside us. It provides a way to look at yourself clearly. It teaches us how to breathe consciously, how to find inner peace, joy and happiness, and how to be patient.

At the beginning, my experiences in the extracorporeal plane, astral trips, and deep meditation seemed sporadic, random things. Complete magic. Some were beautiful, others dark. I remember feeling as though I had been launched into space, extracted from my body while my mind and ego appeared to dissolve. The perception of my being and of reality completely vanished. There was whiteness, light, peace. And in this immense emptiness where nothing existed, I recognized the feeling of being home. Going home was indescribable; there was order and balance. There was no positive or negative, no evil; there was no moral judgment or right and wrong. All was well because everything had already happened.

The experience of living seen through the lens of Otac has allowed me to see things with greater clarity. I have known a complete "love of creation." When I see myself reflected in the All, I feel included in something far greater than this game of "me" and my ego. I realize that I am absolute.

In a now distant past, I once lived under the shadow of injustice. Greed, deceit, and violence dominated everything, and everything was the same. Suffering was seen as something normal and was even a path to salvation and knowing. "No

pain, no gain." Chaos and disorder were normal parts of life.
Misinformation, terrible influences, and general ignorance
governed my world. I even thought that was how it had to
be. Distant are the days when I wandered aimlessly, lost in
the immensity of my solitude and injustice. Then everything
changed and I realized how great was my heart. There was
a mysterious hand at work in my life. I had spent my life
looking for understanding elsewhere: in books, the outside
world, in space. Now I began looking for more of myself, and
for what may be called God. I searched in heaven, in church,
in the figures of saints and preachers and religion, in dogma
and doctrine. I looked and looked, and all I did was fill my
head with dates and facts, name and events, history, geography, art, science fiction, and so on. I found no answers, just
questions. I looked everywhere, and the result was the same.

But twelve years ago on the beaches of Maruata in
Michoacan, mixing mescaline and Salvinorin A in high
doses, I lived an event that proposed a perfect solution.
Since then I have acknowledged that there is indeed a
higher power. We all come from the same place and will
go back to it. Existence is without a doubt a beautiful gift.
I had underappreciated it when I thought life was some
random occurrence that had happened "just because."

Now I knew that "it" was everywhere and that it had
always existed. I just hadn't seen it. I saw that "it" lived and

swam in all the cells of my body, in the cells of everybody including those life-forms without cells. We are all part of a grand living organism.

Nothing I did in my life even remotely reached the level I attained with psychoactive plants; not graduating from school, or my first sexual experience, nor any of the toys I bought along the way, compared to what I eventually discovered. With time and patience, I have attained the wisdom needed to reach my goals. Nothing has filled me with so much satisfaction as the gifts received from *Bufo alvarius*. Neither ayahuasca, nor peyote, mushrooms, LSD, nor cannabis has the therapeutic benefits that I have found in that profoundly generous toad.

As a scientist, I say clearly that this extraordinary being has in its body the strongest healing medicine I have ever known. I have seen how the vapor of the Otac medicine cures chronic bronchitis, strengthens the immune system, helps treat addiction, and heals the organism. It cures depression. I have seen with my own eyes how people have changed their lives after just one experience with the material offered by the toad's glands. Every day more people benefit from its properties. The effects are instantaneous and positive in the short-, medium- and long-term. I feel blessed and privileged. I see this as the most precious gift I could possibly have received.

A New Way of Seeing and Doing

Everything that exists undoubtedly comes from somewhere, but we may not know how to see it because we aren't aware of what lies within. However, it appears to me that sacred plants and the Otac have a property that allows us to access this information. To contemplate it, know it, and feel it is worthy of trust and celebration.

Neurotransmitters, these natural chemical substances found in our brains, function as a chemical link between ourselves and other living beings including plants and "lower" animals. These substances provide us with an entrance to another reality, the world of spirits that arise from the creator, our source of infinite intelligence and true love. We come from, are in, and are returning there. That place is at the center of all creation, and of my soul, and of a flower, and of you. It is within yet beyond dreaming, astral traveling, and out-of-body experiences. It is the stuff of mystical spiritual ecstasy.

It is in such moments of knowing that I can say unequivocally that the Otac toad containing 5-MeO-DMT was the Aztecs' greatest treasure, just as ayahuasca was for the Incas. The states induced by Otac and sacred plants, along with the many representations of the cosmic or feathered serpent in various Mesoamerican cultures, lead me to theorize that we are all Quetzalcoatl, which lives really in our hearts and below our feet. The ancient technologies are the origin and the source of our intelligence and our resistence. I believe there is a connection between human intelligence and entheogens. The time for the return of the cosmic serpent and the energies of these ancient gods is now. The true meanings of many of the teachings of the past are connected with the evolution of our species because they are already there in nature and inside of us, due to our interaction with those energies that have existed for a long time. The ancient knowledge of the Mesoamerican people who venerate the Quezalquoatl feathered serpent is the code and the chemical language that nature has used since the beginning of time.

ADDICTION

In my travels through the Sonora Desert, and then later throughout the world, it has become clear to me that addiction to synthetic substances poses a significant threat to the future of our species. And, based on my experiences as a scientist and a healer, I believe fully that 5-MEo-DMT can provide a crucial tool in the struggle to rescue oneself from addiction.

Synthetic substances such as meth become a mental health problem at a worldwide level. Factors that profoundly alter the evolutionary models of the human condition lead us to social destruction and loss of values and health. In my investigation I can bear witness that there is, in fact, a clinical, medical, and practical application to employ the curative properties of these substances found in nature.

Despite some people verbalizing their desire to abandon addictive behaviors, and their sincere intention to do so, their subsequent behaviors are frequently quite the opposite. Much of this can be explained by chemical processes in the brain. Drug use can lead to internal biochemical processes being completely altered, sometimes irreversibly, due to the extreme outer stimulation of cerebral receptors designed for certain neurotransmitters. Such is the case with dopamine in the use of certain synthetic drugs, or the chemical stimulant

of crystal meth. The entactogens are substances that break
normal psychic defense mechanisms, thus provoking
many serious problems including those concerning
interpersonal relationships.

Drugs have penetrated communities around the world,
including the Seri, causing serious damage to physical and
mental health and impoverishing the quality of life for
families caught up in this intricate web of corruption and
confusion. There is ruthless greed for controlling the human
mind, even enslavement of the mind. It is due to the present
need for a change in human consciousness that the Otac
Foundation has come together. This nonprofit civil associa-
tion is for the conservation, study, investigation, promotion,
comprehension, and development of integral information
centers, schools, and eco-towns in which life is lived free
of our many social cancers, using the ancient plants of the
world, leading to an exchange of knowledge and possibilities at a new, higher level.

I remember reading that the first case of cocaine-induced
psychosis was a student of Freud's. The doctor had
suggested to the student that he begin using cocaine to
help him stop using opium and alcohol. Instead, he became
addicted to all three, and it cost him his sanity. While things
in their natural state may be harmful, far more dangerous
are processed and refined substances.

There is no such thing as overdosing on opium as such. People do not die directly due to the use of opium or morphine when used in its natural state. What happens is that people don't get up to eat and take care of themselves, therefore die of malnutrition, dehydration, or some other cause. And yet how many people have lost their lives due to overdosing on heroin, a powerful derivative of opium? It's the same with cocaine. From a hundred eighty leaves of the coca tree, you get approximately one gram of cocaine. There is no one who can ingest that many leaves. But anyone who is addicted to cocaine, who is already locked into that cycle of horror and degeneration, can easily consume ten grams of it — or even more.

One of our biggest problems is the development of more potent substances that are easier to transport and produce bigger profits for distributors. For example, crystal meth is one of the most addictive and destructive stimulants ever. In a very short amount of time, its effects wreak havoc such as mental disturbances and weight loss that leave the consumer looking like a skin-covered skeleton. There is sisa, a cheap (two euros) and highly destructive methamphetamine used in Greece that may kill the addict just six months after the first use. The cost of this kind of addiction has repercussions on all levels — personal, familial, and social. It is a public health crisis all across the world. It affects the family, productivity, and the economy; therefore, we must focus our energies on understanding and resolving these issues from the very root.

At some level, every human is addicted to something: sex, money, power, exercise, video games, shopping, work, and so on. In fact, we can become addicted to anything that makes us feel any kind of pleasure. We try to replicate the feeling of wellbeing with as much frequency as possible until it consumes the body and our available time. Little by little, we stop doing everything else and the person becomes enslaved by the vice. Of course, it is not the same thing to read the newspaper with one or two cups of coffee a day, compared to smoking methamphetamine, but we're still talking about addiction.

Every day there are new and more destructive drugs. For example, oxi is a cheaper cocaine derivative that's more addictive than crack. Brazil, Peru, Bolivia, and other countries of Central and South American are now being inundated by this terrible drug, with the aid of forces that want to control these populations. Oxi (meaning "oxidated") is a much cheaper derivative of the basic cocaine paste. The drug cartels use the cheapest precursors of the poorest quality; as a consequence, the resulting drug is even more harmful. It is said that four out of every ten oxi consumers die within the first year of use. The potential damage of this drug on a worldwide level is bone-chilling. Kerosene, gasoline, and crude lime are the basic ingredients for this drug. The smoke that is released upon combustion, unlike the white smoke that comes from a crack rock, is grayish white and is said to have 100% addictive potential. That is, everyone who tries it gets hooked on it.

It is alarming to what extremes we've gone, and I'd rather not even think about the consequences if necessary measures are not taken. But I believe we are approaching a key moment in the history of humanity. Today we have the opportunity to change the course of history. We have reached the point where we are all realizing that things must be very different in order to be better. What we need is for something or someone to show us the way out and for all of us to see the necessary path to reach the understanding already achieved by other forms of beings. We must begin to share beautiful things, to hear beautiful stories, for, as we know, not all is death and destruction. But what we can no longer do is ignore the situation and play the ostrich, hiding our heads and believing that nothing is happening. The responsibility belongs to us all.

Action and Movement Generate
Constant Evolution

It is paradoxical that the answer lies here at the border of a land where people have lost so much of their lives and freedom due to illegal drugs. At the level of my own story, I find irony and humor in the relationship between my physical health, my energetic balance, my spiritual awakening, and a borderland desert jewel in one of the most conflicted areas of the planet, the border between Mexico and the United States.

I am presenting you with the gift of rebirth, resuscitation, and reincarnation, from death to life. Thank you, Light Toad. Thank you, Eternal Love. Before their assistance, desolation was my companion. I was imprisoned by my learned habits and the ways encouraged by a consumerist and deceitful society. These factors, added to my inexperience, youth, ignorance, and foolishness, together made for a ticking time bomb and a progressive poisoning of mind, body, and spirit.

How close I was to becoming a zombie forever, like so many who wander the streets asking for money to "eat." Actually, that "eating" means feeding the monster we have created and continue to host within ourselves. It is that voracious insatiable appetite that causes the addiction that enslaves us.

Destiny, to a certain extent, is always unsure. We know we are moving forward; yet time is circular. We must enjoy the journey without focusing on the destination. The point of life is you. When you supposedly lose control of supposed reality, you see your life flash before your eyes. You think about your loved ones, and though you may cry, scream, or laugh, before you even realize it you are no longer there. Suddenly you're filled with an incandescent light expanding from the center of your head. This is the activation of primal processes that connect us with all of creation. It is the recognition of spirit and mind as two entities that coexist in one physical body. Another reality that we do not normally accept due to our limited perception is the millennial medicine used by the most ancient human cultures. It is a safe two-way path to another world, another life, the world of the spirits. As a medicine man, a spiritual being just like you, I live a human story. Each of us writes and narrates his or her own adventure. Every day we forge the future as we draw closer to home.

"What? What are you talking about?" "How is all this even possible?" some might ask. Well, every story has a beginning, and for me it was the toad I kissed that helped me become the prince of my dreams. I had always related to that fairy tale of diamond-encrusted castles, gigantic sparklers, dragons, wizards, and all kinds of larger-than-life characters. Such tales are not unreal at all for they come from the imagination of the eternal and infinite universe. The power of the non-ordinary inhabits these strange lands and dream worlds, which are the only ones that exist. Not the other one, in which we are all alone in a vast, empty universe in which we have to pay for everything: to be born, to eat, to die, to get married, to study, to be happy.

What waits to be discovered within us is beauty itself. It is a better, truer vision. The mind can catapult us to states of supreme pleasure and overwhelming memories that remain for the rest of our days. I believe that the true state of humans is to be, not distant from Eden and suffering, but close to the tree of knowledge, to our history, to our true roots, discovering that the true medicine we need is produced by our own bodies.

We come from nature. We are creation itself, the universe itself. We are made from the primal elements of the cosmos. It is this very cosmos that lives in our bodies. How can we deny the connection between our primordial functions and those of the world that surrounds us? Personal experience of the divine may require many years in a monastery — if it occurs at all — or we can muster the mental flexibility to try conscious breathing. Such work, directed and supported by initiated masters, can be vastly aided by administration of the vapors found in the secretions of the glands of the Otac.

OTAC SAVING LIVES

Each person has a unique experience with the Sonora toad, but with similar results: they find peace and well-being at the end of the journey. I remember the typical Ravers from the old days of rock concerts, totally intoxicated with multiple chemical substances that stressed and increasingly emaciated their bodies. The rumor of Otac spread fast in such circles of people that included DJs and musicians. Such people were experts in drugs and hallucinogens, but no one could believe that something so small could show us so much of the universe in so little time. There was a general feeling of perplexity.

And so, without further ado, I took my belongings and embarked on the biggest journey yet: reinventing myself as an individual and pursuing my dreams supported by the greatest energies I had yet known. There was cosmic consciousness beating in my heart, and within the perfect biological design of my cells danced a rhythm of perfection. I felt beauty, harmony, and total comprehension. Within a few years of honest hard work, in which I enjoyed the process of spiritual purification and energy synchroniza- tion with creation, I developed a technique for the proper management of the 5MeO-DMT pyrolysis (thermochemical extraction).

My associates and I began to videotape Otac sessions,
and about sixty such sessions caught on tape resemble, in
some cases, exorcisms taken from a horror movie. Others
are quite placid in appearance. But, in the end, most agree
on the benefits of this extraordinary experience. With the
help of brothers Ogarrio Perkins and Odily Fuentes, who
have been working with the Comca'ac (another name for
the Seri people) for more than twenty years, I was able to
approach them.

Being that the *Bufo alvarius* is an endemic species with
unique properties, I thought that the people longest in the
region would have knowledge of it, but as the years passed
I realized that was not so, or at least if it had been, the
information has not been preserved over time. During the
four years that I lived in Hermosillo while investigating
the 5MeO- DMT molecule, I was unable to find information about its medicinal use in Sonora. Regardless, the most
complete work that I found during my last investigation
was that of James Oroc in his book *Tryptamine Palace*
where he writes a description of his personal experiences
with *Bufo alvarius* and the positive changes that came about
in his life due to the medicinal properties found in the
substance. Because of that, I decided to begin the necessary
work toward a scientific and spiritual comprehension of the
therapeutic use of the substance from found information,

intuition, and praxis with the help of Odily Fuentes and Roberto Perkins.

Odily Fuentes is an art editor, painter, and sculptor whose work is greatly inspired by the teachings of Comca'ac shamans. Roberto has been working with the use of the plants of power as tools of knowledge and contemplation for more than twenty years. When I met them, Fuentes and Perkins were just arriving from the Peruvian Amazon after having participated in ayahuasca ceremonies. Ayahuasca contains varieties of the active substance in DMT (dimethyl-tryptamine), as does the Otac. In this particular case, it is N, N-DMT.

It was with Carlos Ernesto Ogarrio Perkins, an academic at the University of Sonora, that I arrived at this community, as that university had a longstanding relationship with the Comca'ac. I offered them the medicine, the offering of the toad, and right away they felt that it was both natural and extremely powerful. They understood me perfectly and felt a need to channel the use of the medicine toward more concrete ends than just experimenting with altered states of consciousness. All this might seem like a huge coincidence, but to me it was as if everything were mathematically destined. A high intelligence is involved in this work, and if it is pursued in an impeccable manner, it can bring health to many people.

Healing for the Seri: Case Studies

The Comca'ac people have resisted and adapted to many forced changes during their history. As these changes have been implemented with little planning or adaptation to the needs of the community, this has led to severe damage on social and ecological levels. To date, they keep on coming up against the most destructive vices of modernity, the exploitation and depletion of their natural resources, along with junk food and designer drugs like meth. Families are disjointed and the autonomy of the people is weakened due to the disproportionately high ambition of their communal leaders. The traditional authority, the Head of the Council of Elders, can do nothing against this at all and even accepts it as the death of his culture.

It has been very rewarding to implement with the Comca'ac an entirely scientific and practical study applying holistic healing through rechanneling the energetic centers of the body. That is to say, both health and wellness are emotional states that have a lot to do with the processes of the mind. Regardless of the severity of a physical illness, if there is spiritual tranquility, then the quality of life can increase. Therefore, what we are to understand is that health is the balance and equilibrium of all the biochemical processes in the body, which are intimately related to the external environment.

Case Study: Raymundo

The first Kunkak patient was Raymundo, who back then worked for the government in his community. He was forty-three years old and he'd been dealing with a longtime use of methamphetamines. His propensity to smoke the drug pushed him to leave his job. His family had abandoned him and he had even wanted to commit suicide. In a desperate attempt to get help, he asked for a loan and traveled to Hermosillo. He looked for his friend, Carlos, the scholar at the University of Sonora, and with whom he had worked on a compilation of Comca'ac traditional songs as a translator. Carlos, seeing him in such a state, called me, and that night I went with my assistant to perform the first modern healing on a native of Sonora, the home of the mythical *Bufo alvarius.*

When I reached his home, after greeting those present, I was introduced to the patient. Raymundo looked exhausted, and his face was full of sadness. I squeezed his hand and gave him a hug and told him everything was going to be okay. I gave him instructions in regard to his breathing. The lights were turned off and the songs of grandfather Miguel were playing in the background. The healing began. With three intense inhalations of the sacred vapors, he immediately felt the effects. He lay down, threw up a bit, and, after a few minutes, said he felt better. We repeated this three times in one night. At the end, Raymundo looked happy and said he was hungry.

That week we were invited to the Punta Chueca community to give our first healing ceremony. It was attended by Ursula, Panchito's wife, the son of the legendary "Chapo" Barnett; and Raymundo's brother, plus five other people. Some of the men of the tribe and other Yoris or Corzars were also present, what the Comca'ac call "Mexican and foreign visitors."

It was a beautiful day for healing, and the focus was Miguel, the relative of a member of the Council of Elders. What followed was a very intense therapy in which I observed for the first time the inverted-hands position that people naturally go into when they've had a very strong dose of 5-MeO-DMT. It was like the images that my uncle had seen, as had the archeologist Jose Francisco Hinojosa, of Mayan effigies showing that same position, replicating the feet of a frog.

After having done said therapy, and with the Seri authorization at hand, we decided to have a ceremony of initiation inside a nearby pyramid. It was a megalithic structure composed of two rocks leaning against each other, situated in a strategic place. It was a type of observatory and a lookout point. The pyramid was and is a sacred place for the Comca'ac, which is why few people have known about it.

To reach the pyramid, one must walk uphill for about fifteen minutes. The view is truly beautiful from up there. You can see the island and the "canal from hell." When we began to climb, it immediately started to rain, which made us quicken our steps. When we got to the structure, it was as if we had gone back to prehistoric times. Raymundo and his friends accompanied us. Once inside, we all did one inhalation of the Otac molecule. It was a collective experience of strength, guided by Raymundo's songs. In the end, I decided to do it once on my own. It was one of the most beautiful psycho-integrative experiences I've ever had. That is where and when I began to learn "Song of the Fog."

Xeele cooal iya, hant it hant ia
Tiix compisaiix

When we finished the session and I came out of the pyramid, I felt like a new man, stronger and more sure of myself. I have been nothing but blessed by having found the original territorial inhabitants of this magic.

That day, energetic portals opened in front of our eyes. We saw that light flows like an endless spring, carrying health, energy, and love to all of the world's inhabitants who desire it. From that moment, one of the most important

stages in the history of the Otac movement was sealed: the
return of ancestral healing to its true home. With the aid
of my friends, I prepared an entire program for community
assistance that revolved around the use of such powerful
medicine. Upon entering the community, Raymundo, who
is already very much recovered, converted a piece of land
into living quarters and a clinic. The cousin of Carlos and
Xixi (Luis), Jesús Ogarrio Huitrón, arrived during that
time. A sociologist, Jesús came to write his thesis about the
Comca'ac. He has trained in ancestral songs and initiation
ceremonies for the purpose of comprehending nature. He
was, without a doubt, an important part of this project. He
joined after the first session of 5-MeO-DMT, and his thesis
presented the first written reference to the work that I've
carried out with the Seris.

The first thing that I asked Raymundo about was the name
of the little toad in a place called Quimique itom and he
responded, "Ziij hax anox quijiix," which means "Thing that
sits upon the water." I was lent a copy of the Seri-Spanish-
English dictionary during my first visit to the Kunkak
territory. Much to my surprise, upon initially opening the
dictionary to a random page, I saw the figure of the little
toad along with the word *Otac*. Its definition described
Otac as something taboo. The name of Otac in the public
life of our society resurfaced from there. From that moment
on, Jesús began to document the events that occurred during

those months in a territory that was carefully defended against white invasion. For me that cultural experience was an honor, an enormous privilege, and an opportunity to learn many new things such as their songs, and the magic of nature. I was able to share with those beautiful people what I had learned traveling this world, and enhance my knowledge with the timeless wisdom of these tribes and their invaluable knowledge unknown in commercial and consumerist modernity.

That year there were three celebrations given for the Leatherback Turtle, after more than thirty years without a celebration. Being present for these festivities in the community truly filled me with satisfaction. All of the Comca'ac are very friendly. In the middle of the star-filled sky, with Shark Island at my back, I greeted the attendees. Among the elders was the head of the council, Sir Antonio Robles, who was always accompanied by Raymundo. I took part in the traditional foods such as Seri bread, Loggerhead Sea Turtle (Mossni), and mule deer venison, all real delicacies of the kind that you may get to sample once in a lifetime.

Case Study: Miguel

Among the cases that I remember frequently is that of Miguel, who was twenty-two years old and father to a young child. Back then, Miguel was an intense user of heroin, but after the nightly toad therapy, he decided to put himself through rehab. Now after two years of not using, he has successfully reincorporated himself into society. Miguel has overcome his addiction. He is a living example of the healing capacity of toad medicine. His first session with bufotenin is only remembered by Miguel, my girlfriend, and myself. We had to find the place, and prepare the patient and healing material. We created an inspiring ritual involving the patient himself and then, after smoking, a series of changes began: the coloring of his skin went from pale to green then purple; he stopped breathing for about two seconds then began to vomit a brown, gelatinous material. He was squirming and screaming so violently, his body contorting, that I was afraid.

When Miguel began to calm down and return from his trip, he had an entirely different look on his face. There was a new light in his eyes. He asked me if he could do it again, right then and there. I agreed. Miguel confessed that, despite the intensity of the experience, he hadn't been able to completely let himself go because something kept him anchored to reality.

Reaching down, Miguel removed the sole from his shoe and pulled out a hypodermic syringe and a plastic-wrapped dose of heroin. After discarding it, Miguel smoked again. The second trip was much more intense. He felt a strong sense of freedom and relief from the oppression of his addiction. Miguel decided to go into rehab, and was eventually sucessful in overcoming his addiction. As you probably know, heroin is one of the most difficult addictions to treat, even in the best clinics and rehabilitation centers.

Draw your own conclusions.

Case Study: Sir Francisco

In the days just after my arrival among the Seri, more brave souls began to appear to take the little toad medicine. They were people who respected the medicine because Miguel had been cured. Everyone in the area knew that toad medicine wasn't a game. Among the many people who circulated in front of the laboratory's Bunsen burner was Sir Francisco, who was a shaman and a traditional doctor. He had been away on a trip to Arizona when I originally arrived in the community. Being a man of knowledge who had traveled the world, he knew about ancestral medicines. It was a complete honor for me to be able to teach him the most profound secrets of his own land.

In his first session, Sir Francisco breathed in the molecules then, seconds after beginning the trip, when everything was still very intense, he opened his eyes, stood up, and went out walking, as if nothing were happening. When I later asked him why he'd left during the session, his response was wise, as one would expect of a powerful man such as himself:

"Yes, it is very beautiful up there with the spirits, but it's not for strolling around nor meandering about. The moment that you arrive, you see and you know what you need to know, and then you come back to work because here is where there are a lot of things to do. People want to stay there looking around and getting to know the place. We are from there, and we will return there, and I am no longer in a hurry. I now know."

Sir Francisco's words left me stunned. There was complete truth in his words. This elder showed me many things, among them that he was already familiar with the expanded state before having tried the Otac. It was nothing out of the ordinary for him to feel what lies beyond.

I was extremely excited. Over the following days, Sir Francisco demonstrated his power to me and gave me a gift. He taught me a few songs. They were the first that I learned from him: "The Song of the Wind" and "The Song of Power." When he sang them to me, I was transported to other times through the vibration of the sounds. It's truly magical what these people do, they who have inherited the power through their ancestors taught by Mother Nature herself.

Case Study: Don Antonio Robles, Chief of the Elderly
The visit from the chief of the Council of the Elderly, Antonio Robles, and his wife, Mrs. Ramona Barnett Astorga, was memorable. They are some of the wisest people in the community. Sir Antonio and his wife seemed very worried about the situation faced by their community. He, especially, looked exhausted. He seemed to be carrying all the pain of his family and community on his back.

After being given the instructions about inhaling the medicinal vapors of the Otac, Don Antonio was more than ready. The moment he had the pipe in his hands, the chief took a very deep breath. He held the medicine in his body the indicated amount of time and, little by little, began to exhale it. Immediately he became rigid and felt the power of the medicine. His expression began to change, and each moment he looked more relaxed and his breathing became more tranquil. But he didn't want to lie down. I noticed a certain resistance against the cosmic impulse that the toad molecule gives you. He was being cured, but in his own manner. His spirit was manifesting.

Case Study: Ramona Barnett Astorga

Shortly thereafter, we began to feel a powerful energy emanating from the elderly couple. The complex compositions of the songs of Mrs. Ramona were transporting us to another dimension. The harmonizing articulation of each note was giving us access to a most profound plane of consciousness where the wise woman was our guide between worlds. Soon, it seemed as if the small room would either explode or take off flying. The amount of concentrated power there was highly significant. The ceremony was almost finished when Mrs. Ramona stopped singing and became still but still in a state of concentration. The chief stood up and said that he felt much better, more relaxed and stronger. Picking up their things, the couple gave us thanks and said their good-byes.

Case Study: Margarito

Then came the healing of a young Comca'ac named
Margarito, Sir Francisco's son. He already knew the instructions and was ready to be cured. With a good dosage of
the little toad, the young Comca'ac began his treatment
with comforting words and a Tibetan singing bowl (which
I used before learning the songs that I have since used).
Margarito had all of the will to cure himself and become a
better person. We watched him fight for at least two hours,
going up against his inner darkness with great valor. I must
confess that seeing his process from the outside was horri-
fying. In many cases, vomit is the physical form of expulsion
of everything unhealthy. His was gelatinous and greenish
in color. It was not food. The medicine, combined with the
vibrations of the Tibetan bowl, created a powerful reaction
upon each atom of Margarito's body.

After the first fifteen minutes, he requested more medicine
because there was still so much filth inside his being, and
he wanted to do away with it permanently. Another strong
dose of the little toad was prepared for him, and it had the
same powerfully purifying effects. In moments such as that,
it is important to demonstrate assistance, comprehension, and
above all much affection for the patient. These are fundamental elements for healing, and these attentions were made
available to this young Comca'ac. After three strong doses of
5MeO-DMT, Margarito said that he felt lighter and much
better, which was truly reflected by his smiling face. The
medicine of the Otac had once more shown its healing power.

The Impassioned Words of Raymundo

"This place was very sacred to my ancestors. Here behind the bush is an ancient cemetery of the wise men of the mountains, those who walked to live. They are the ones we came to visit and honor. We are going to offer our demons to them. We came to ask their permission to use the little toad, because using it well is the task of a well-aligned soul and mind. We need the blessing of the grandparents, so we are going to walk so that all of them see us."

Walking in the sacred places is heavier than normal, you feel a very strong energy, there is a force that commands you to walk erect and to walk with strong and sure steps in order to not fall. The freezing wind penetrates your jacket and layered clothes and pushes you with little gusts. That strength in its moment represented peace, like cold caresses from the wind that won't kill you if you are respectful of the ground you walk upon.

The ceremony began once we arrived at the fire pit. It was about combining the phenethylamine of hikuli (peyote) with the powerful medicine of the Otac on sacred ground. Next to a native, our guide began to say, "This song came to me fifteen years ago, the day I left my house very early to walk in the desert and on the mountain. When the Lord Sun came out, he gave me this song as a gift. He talks about the food we receive from his rays when they enter us:

Zaah (Sun)

Zaah (Sun)

Zaah, zaah, tameepit iya Zaah

Zaah, zaah, tameepit iya Zaah

Temeepit iya Zaah inööj iya

Hant com cöpooft iya

Hant hac siima xöee..."

Sun

Sun, Sun, the entrance to the astounding.

Sun, Sun, the entrance to the astounding

In the Sun there is a place, an entrance

If I can get to the entrance to this place

This place will be my dwelling where I shall rest....

"Watch as the dew falls on the mangrove tree," Raymundo said. "Someone wrote the song Xeele Coal ("Song of the Fog") because of that. Because it is pure life. It says that in this life you're going to have, of that which you see, of those droplets, the ones that later are transformed into food inside the plants when you give them rays of sun. That is what you people call photosynthesis, the food that makes the plants grow, that we eat. Because that food doesn't just go to our bellies; oxygen is also our nourishment and our connection to all of the processes of life and consciousness. So, always breathe in deeply. It's like my grandfather taught me... "

Xeele Coaal

Xeele coaal iya hant it hant yaat
quiisaj iti momatoj iya...

Song to the Fog

I'm going to take all of the filth
of my mind and of my body
and discard it here
Let's go
I'm not the only one who needs to be cleansed.
Sing with me!...
Xeele coaal iya...
We can do this!"

And we sang:

Xeele coaal iya hant it hant yaat

Iquiisaj iti momatoj iya Xeele coal iya hant it hant yaat
Iquiisaj iti momatoj iya Xeele coal iya hant it hant yaat

Iquiisaj iti momatoj iya

Tiix compiisax iya tiix compiisax Tiix compiisax iya tiix
compiisax Iquiisaj iti moyatoj iya...

Where the dew falls, springs life;
where the dew falls, springs life;
where the dew falls, springs life;
You should drink from that life
you will have of that life

We sang until the moon was above our heads. I could certainly feel the magnetic power of the moon. I couldn't stop looking. It was genuinely a mystical experience. The moon passes, reflects the light, and is amazed by what it sees in its path. We admire its beauty, but those beings also are amazed by us where we are. Because of that, the moon itself sings:

HANT IHYAAO IYA

Hamiime ihyaao iya
Hant ihyaao iya
Tameepit iya...

SONG OF THE MOON

Where I pass
Path in the sky
Where I pass is amazing...

When he finished singing, Raymundo said, "Thank you, Grandfather. Wherever you are, help us and send us your blessings to convince the people to purify themselves. I like you; this is why I sing to you. That's what my grandfather would say." Raymundo took the Tibetan bowl and hit it a few times. Each time he struck it with more concentration. The sounds were more and more perfect, and the master was able to make the foreign instrument sing in the tongue of the Comca'ac.

Suddenly Raymundo told me, "Doc, you've already cured me. Now I'm going to give you a gift from my ancestors. Lean back and close your eyes."

He began to move his hands over my body and my head. He did a combination of songs and movements that I had never seen or heard before. The voice of the shaman began to change and afterward his appearance. He had been transformed into an old man and then into other creatures. His movements and songs became a powerful circular dance around my body. Numerous fears invaded my body and, at the end of the ritual, I felt completely free of them. It was the last time I ever felt them.

A soft, icy breeze entered and left my body in the form of a spiral. I tried to think as little as possible, actually not at all. The shaman was working. "Without mind, without ideas, without complications… No pressures!" said Raymundo, who began to sway unsteadily.

"That is the magic, my brothers. It's just pure life. Life that goes beyond what we see. We are going to keep singing because this is very much about will. We cannot sleep now."

By then we knew more songs, and the attention and concentration that was required was enough to unite our voices with that of the master and become a single one. Each stanza was one step closer to eternity, to the supreme conscience. The power of nature, life and harmony in its ultimate expression, was revealed to us through the vocalization of this ancient knowledge. Nature showed us her magic without any exotic visions because we showed our honor to her and to all of the beings. There was no longer sleepiness or fatigue.

My Wish for the World: Only Peace and Joy

As a result of my personal exploration with the Otac, and my efforts to share the toad medicine with thousands of people throughout the world, I've come to realize how much I want the endless light of the ultimate love to reign forever, as we have known in the past, and to honor that to which honor is due. There are things both sacred and beautiful that are beyond business or profit, which are relics of an obsolete system. I want for there to be respect toward Mother Nature and for every living being. No more pain, hunger, or searching. It is time for us to become responsible.

I invite you to begin your path to divinity today. I am proposing that you simply know, simply be, simply travel forward moment by moment. I am talking about having fun together once we have forgiven our past, once we have recognized our mistakes and returned to our true state: perfect machines that host life. There are more bacteria living on a single adult human than there are people on the face of the Earth. We are universes within ourselves, as vast as our imagination can allow, even in our highest states of perception.

This is heaven on earth, and it's earth in heaven, fusing our souls with matter as we return to our origin, level zero, our parting point and from there to infinity. There are no limits to consciousness or reason. They are ancient prophecies now manifest. Rejoice, love, and be joyful. Don't ask if this is possible because it happened yesterday, it is happening today, and it will happen tomorrow, on and on until we become forever itself. Until we erase from memory any pain that may have been experienced. We sow light if we teach based on truth and not on lies or half-truths manipulated for interests not at all related to what truly matters. A peaceful world is possible within humanity's timeline. Everyone living in harmony, together as brothers and sisters.

The only ideal that truly works is nature's consciousness, the spiritual wise man and woman, the ancient shaman with total understanding of everything, of continuous peace and absolute perfection. I choose to follow my inner voice. I choose to trust internal, millennial, and ancestral intuition. And once again today I decide to change the path my life has taken, reinventing myself, exploring parts of myself I did not know before, that bring me a little closer each time to the beginning. If life has been this good up until now, I can't imagine how magnificent the next destination will be.

I live in heaven in this moment. Things happen, and everything I need is supplied. New forms of life are surging where no signs existed before. After the darkest struggle I could possibly have faced, I gave in, began controlling my impulses, and found my balance. I retook my rightful place as master of my universe.

Those European explorers entranced by gold, those who chased after the shiny metal, those who were told about El Dorado, the Incas' most beautiful jungle city — those people didn't realize that the Incas were referring to ayahuasca. The Aztecs' greatest treasure, too, was something other than gold. Indeed there is nothing, or at least very little, more sacred than the holy substance given by the Otac toad. The reason why gold was valuable for Mesoamericans, Egyptians, and other ancient cultures was its similitude in brightness to the sun and to the states experienced through sacred medicine, magical states that open up other realities. A wisdom state is produced by the plants themselves, and the obvious relationship between one thing and another, is revealed.

The time has come for all of us to meet our destiny. Humanity's destiny is already set. There are no new continents to discover. Now everything comes from beyond geography, from another world. Despite our strange way of seeing life. Despite our misunderstanding. Despite our poor capacity to follow clues left by the spirit walkers of the past, abandoned and forgotten in the darkness of a long, sad night. They are gone, the walkers of all paths, the masters of time, but their voices still echo.

The resurgence of the godlike toad must give us the drive to gain legalization for Otac and medicinal plants (mushrooms, peyote, ayahuasca, etc.) and for the study of other plants with therapeutic potential. We must permit the expansion and exploration of our consciousness and imagination. No more oppression. No more death and deception. I suspect that you, too, are sick and tired of the downward spiral toward destruction due to conformity and mediocrity. Enough confusion.

Let us free the spirit and reach our potential.

Afterword

Notes for Working with the Otac Medicine of the Sonoran Desert Toad

by Maya Larissa

Right now Earth's four winds are blowing upon you. They are all life, health, and well-being for you, so that you can attain a higher knowledge. Nobody can take this away from you because it is a gift, a blessing for you for the rest of your life.

En estos momentos te soplan los cuatro vientos del globo terráqueo. Todos ellos son vida, salud y bienestar para ti; para que adquieras un conocimiento superior. Nada ni nadie te lo va a poder quitar porque esto es un don, un regalo para ti, para el resto de tu vida.

Abuelo Pancho

Seri Elder

PRE-TOAD

Humanity has long sought truth, healing, spiritual awakening, and esoteric exploration through shamanic modalities. Akin to ayahuasca, DMT, peyote, San Pedro, kambo, iboga, yopo, and other traditional shamanic modalities, Otac is now being experienced with immense effect.

Among those who have participated in this ceremonial ritual there is often reference to a "total reset." This is most significantly a holistic reset that allows for a deep release of destructive emotional and mental patterns, as well as an influx of life force that is both inspirational and healing. Partaking in Otac can potentially be a life-changing experience of immense significance.

For wellbeing, it is highly recommended that an initiated guide be with you during your journey. However, even in a supervised environment, remain aware that ultimately *you* are responsible for the benefits you garner and for the way you relate to any challenges you may encounter either during or after the experience. This is not a recreational drug and is certainly not for everybody.

Otac is like no other psychedelic. Do not assume that a background of entheogenic exploration will suffice to take you through this with ease. Otac contains both 5-MeO-DMT and bufotenin, and is infinitely more intense than smoking pure DMT. If you are unclear about this, I highly advise you to do further research before embarking on a journey.

Due to its immense effect, partaking in Otac ought to be seriously considered. Certainly those with psychological problems are to take caution as integrating the effect of this substance can be challenging for even the most stable of minds. Before partaking, assess whether you are willing to hold personal accountability for your actions and the consequences thereof. This is essential for the experience to come to fruition.

The ritual of Otac is a rite of passage. Prepare your body and mind accordingly and consider your intention. A clean vessel and stable mind may allow for greater ease during and after the experience. Letting go the stronghold of the mind is essential when it comes to this unique opportunity. Beneficial transformation ultimately requires your willingness to release all preconceived notions of the nature of reality and of your self-identity.

A well-nourished and rested body with minimal food and water in the system is ideal. The aim is to be conscious, calm, and centered.

Refrain from drug use. Alcohol, SSRIs, and other chemicals in the system can cause adverse reactions that are likely to intensify the experience significantly and potentially make for a challenging outcome. Also, it is not recommened to journey with the toad serum if you are elderly or have been diagnosed with a heart condition or hypertension, due to the resultant accelerated heartbeat. In the case of drug addiction, it is essential that the facilitator be well aware of your circumstances and substance use.

An Otac initiation is wisely considered the beginning of a journey that continues long after the event. This awareness will assist with what may be the most essential aspect of your experience — that of integration.

Post-Toad

Integrating the phenomenon of Otac is an unfolding that must be considered for its ongoing effects. Many people report a sense of clarity, inspiration, and focus. New ways of relating to the world, to others, and to their life purpose are among reported benefits. For the seeker, profound insight is offered regarding the nature of existence and divinity.

Otac is undoubtedly a psychic, spiritual, and emotional cleanser. For some there is a sense that much has been stirred within the psyche and that deeper release is possible. Occasionally it may be suggested by the facilitator that a person return for more, and at other times it is simply a matter of addressing what has been brought to the fore via intentional practice.

Also of significance are recurring waves of the initial experience that may happen at unexpected moments. Though predominantly less intense than the original event, they are just as vital. As Dr. Rettig believes, "these waves are a combination of the body re-creating the experience by producing the molecules naturally, and also part of the gift of the medicine revealing that you can cause the effect by yourself." In time you may find that you are able to initiate reactivation waves via your own conscious intent.

Letting these moments pass through our minds and bodies with acceptance and grace, like when the sun flashes brightly upon our eyes and we relax until the intensity passes, is an art form in itself that invites a further calibration of consciousness to occur. If one struggles during a spontaneous wave, a cycle of tension and reaction may create unnecessary challenge for the individual. In these instances sleep may be challenged and adverse effects may include a sense of instability and inability to cope. If this occurs, exercise, meditation, dance, yoga, and other forms of both exertion and relaxation are recommended. Reaching out for support from others who know what you have partaken in is also advised.

We are all being called to hold a profound degree of self-responsibility. It is also strongly advised that each participant self-reflect to see what they can do for themselves. The desired shift may occur simply by releasing a destructive habit, thought pattern, or offering forgiveness to oneself and others. The practice of gratitude has been shown in neuroscience to significantly activate healing and cognitive refinement. To consider all that you are grateful for is to consciously enhance love and unity with oneself and others, and to inspire body and mind healing. This in turn supports our continued movement toward harmonious living among humanity and upon Gaia.

Of immense benefit is to have experienced caretakers and healers available to assist with integration, and to also be available for follow-up contact.

It is also suggested that micro communities form among those who have experienced Otac. People are reporting the successful formation of private groups for those who have had direct experience in their local area, inviting ongoing communication and support. One very positive outcome in these instances is that individuals who desire support are able to ask for and receive personal attention. These micro communities are an effective way to establish a network that encourages grounded integration, ongoing care, and a healthy point of reflection.

Axatipe!

MAYA LARISSA, *a former moderator on the worldwide Ayahuasca Forum, is a conference speaker with thirteen years of experience in shamanic initiation, training, and facilitation.*

About the Author

DR. OCTAVIO RETTIG HINOJOSA is a Mexican doctor who works with the sacred medicine 5-MeO-DMT found in the secretions of the Sonoran Desert toad (*Bufo alvarius*). Dr. Rettig has worked with the Seri Tribe of Sonora,

Photo by Ivan Cummins

Mexico, to help treat methamphetamine addicts, reintroducing the use of the medicine to the local culture that had lost it. He has learned the ancient songs and rites of the Seri from "Don Pancho," an elder Seri shaman, and has been authorized by the council of Seri elders to use this most powerful of shamanic medicines in the West. Dr. Rettig travels extensively throughout Mexico, the US, Australia, and Europe to give lectures and lead healing ceremonies. He is a member of the active reserve of the UN, working with ANUV as part of the project for indigenous traditional ancient Mezoamerican and Amazonian medicines. He lives in Guadalajara, Mexico. You may contact him on Facebook at Otac el Sapo del Desierto de Sonora, or Octavio Rettig. He may be reached by e-mail at dr.otac@hotmail.com.

RAK RAZAM (Introduction) is a founding editor of *Undergrowth*, Australia's leading alternative arts and literature magazine, and the world's leading experiential journalist, writing about and helping shape the emergence of a new cultural paradigm in the 21st century. He is the author of the critically acclaimed book *Aya: A Shamanic Odyssey* and a frequent lecturer on ayahuasca and the shamanic revival sweeping the West. He lives in Melbourne, Australia.

SANTIAGO PANDO (Preface)
Visual Artisan.
After years in advertising, Santiago Pando changed his view and realized that life's best product isn't meant to be sold, but to be shared. That product is consciousness. His latest film, *RE: Reconexión Natural*, shares this vision through what connects us all: our food and what we eat.

AYAHUASCA

Rituals, Potions and Visionary Art from the Amazon

ARNO ADELAARS, CHRISTIAN RÄTSCH, CLAUDIA MÜLLER-EBELING

The authors are recognized experts in the field of ethnology, anthropology, and pharmacology and demonstrate the use of Ayahuasca in shamanic rituals. They dive deep into shamanic visionary worlds, explore the plants and their souls, and share their authentic encounters with Amazonian cultures and their artistic works.

Christian Rätsch is an ethnologist and ethnopharmacologist, speaker, and author. He is the author of the classic masterwork *The Encyclopedia of Psychoactive Plants.*

Arno Adelaars lives in Amsterdam and has explored psychedelic substances for over 20 years. He works as a freelance journalist and author, and previously as a reporter for Dutch and German news channels.

Claudia Müller-Ebeling is an art historian and ethnologist specializing in visionary art. Over the last 20 years she has written about Korean Shamanism, the Amazon region, and about principles of shamanic art in Nepal.

$29.95 · 310 PAGES · HARCOVER · ISBN 9781611250510

Save 25% at **DIVINEARTSMEDIA**.com | **800 833 5738**

AHAHUASCA JUNGLE VISIONS

A Coloring Book

ALEXANDER GEORGE WARD

Ayahuasca Jungle Visions is a coloring book inspired by artist Alexander Ward's journey from the source of the Amazon River into the very heart of the Amazon Jungle. There, at the home to the greatest abundance of life on this sacred Earth, Ward encountered the ancient cultures and traditions of tribes that have learned to live in harmony with Mother Nature. The magnificent illustrations that grew from his travels call out to be filled with colorful vitality.

Alexander George Ward is a world-traversing, multidisciplinary, visionary artist. He graduated with a Bachelor of Arts degree in traditional animation from the Arts University in Bournemouth and has worked as an art director for the animated feature film *Back to the Sea* (China) and as a conceptual artist for video games such as *DJ Hero 2* (UK). He divides his time between the UK and Greece.

$12.95 · 112 PAGES · ISBN 9781611250534

Transforming self. Celebrating life.

Divine Arts was created five years ago to share some of the new and ancient knowledge that is rapidly emerging from the indigenous and wisdom cultures of the world; and to present new voices that express eternal truths in innovative and accessible ways.

We have realized from the shifts in our own consciousness that millions of people worldwide are simultaneously expanding their awareness and experiencing the multi-dimensional nature of reality.

Our authors, masters and teachers from around the world, have come together from all spiritual practices to create Divine Arts books. Our unity comes in celebrating the sacredness of life, and having the intention that our work will assist in raising our consciousness which will ultimately benefit all sentient beings.

We trust that these books will serve you on whatever path you journey, and we welcome hearing from you.

Michael Wiese and Geraldine Overton,
Publishers

mw@mwp.com   *glow@blue-earth.co.uk*